MAKING WOODEN TOYS

B T Batsford Ltd London

MAKING WOODEN TOYS

Roger Polley

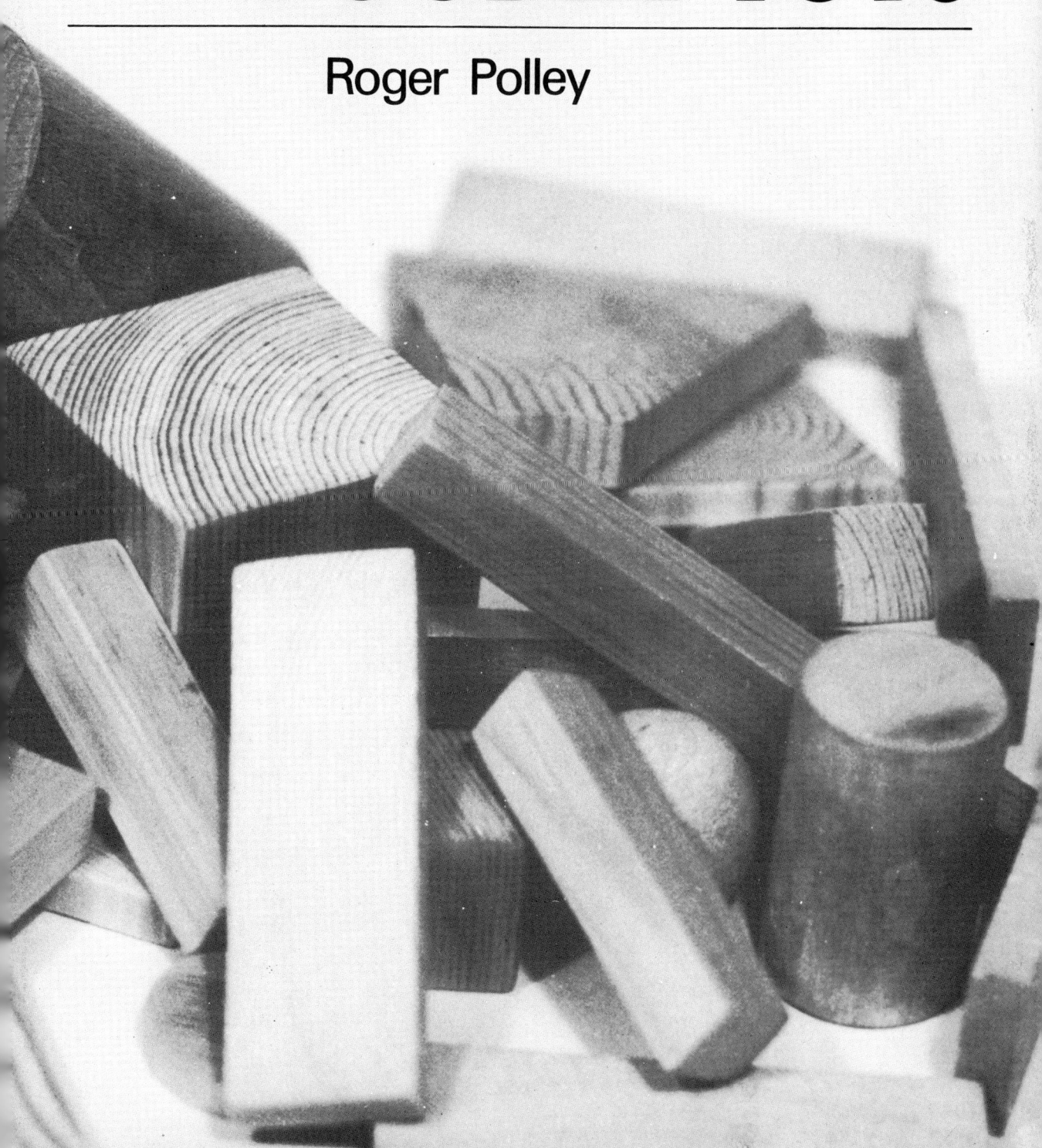

To Em, Vic, Gran, Richard, Keith, Ron, Kevin, Linda, Noel Palmer, Peter Hawkins and all my friends.

ISBN 0 7134 0823 5

Printed in Great Britain by
Cox & Wyman Ltd, Fakenham
for the Publishers B T Batsford Ltd
4 Fitzhardinge Street London W1H 0AH

CONTENTS

Acknowledgment

I would like to thank Linda
Palmer for the line drawings,
retouching, typing the manu-
script, and moral support
throughout this book: also my
good friend Lucy Williams for
the photography with special
help from Bernard.

INTRODUCTION

I would like to think this book will cater for all age groups and people of mixed ability, as well as constituting a form of reference for art and craft teachers. Although the toys and games are designed with children in mind, the puzzles can be enjoyed by both children and adults alike. All the objects are of a functional nature, but some also have a high sculptural content.

You do not need a sophisticated workshop to make these objects, just a small table and some basic tools. The majority of the materials may be bought quite cheaply at any timber yard and hardware shop.

Every project has easy-to-follow text, with alternative suggestions adding some flexibility to each idea. Use the projects as a springboard for your own creativity, and get your mind working on original ideas. No matter how obscure or far-fetched they may be, with a little thought they can usually be made to function. It is useful to keep a small note-book handy to jot down ideas and rough sketches for toys and games that you would like to make at some time in the future.

It is always more rewarding and satisfying to give friends a present that you have personally made, so start creating and surprise yourself!

TOOLBOX

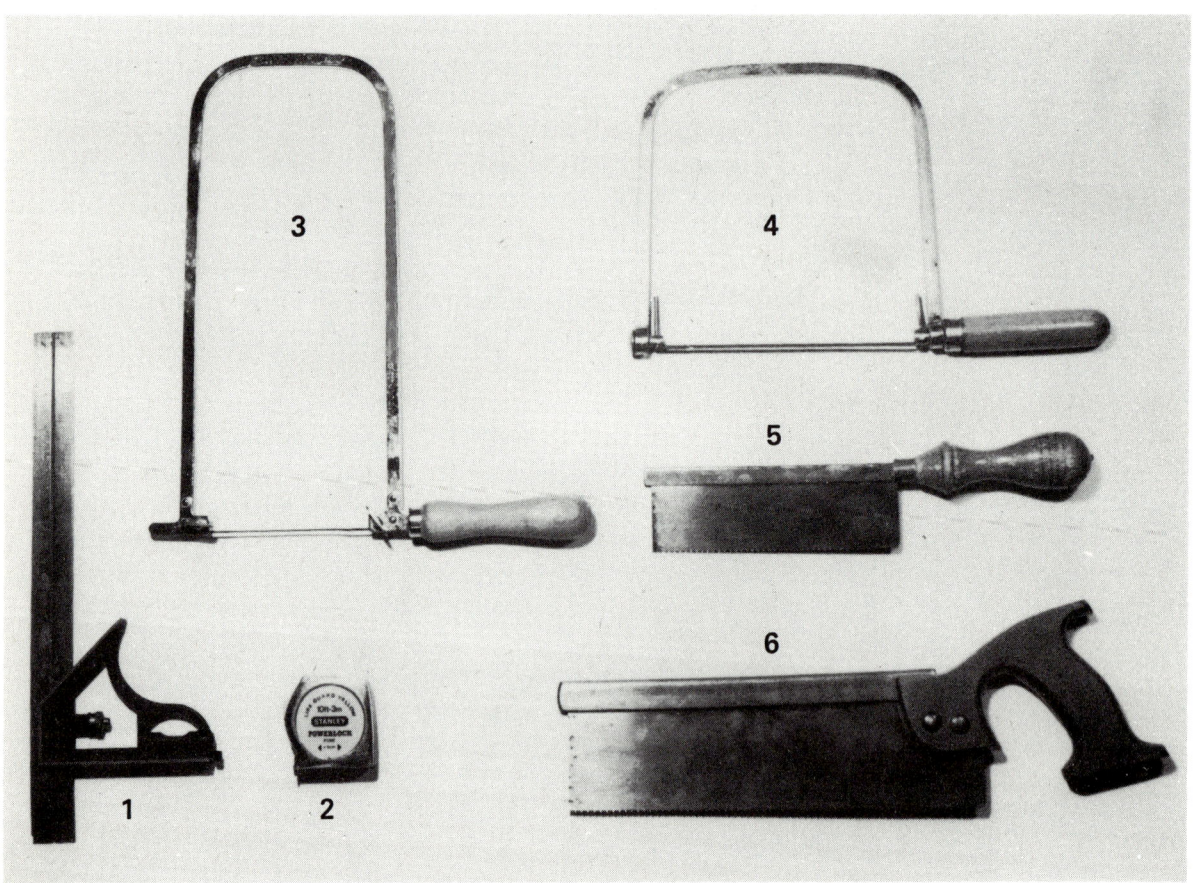

1 *Try-square* used to obtain right-angled cutting lines and for checking that edges and sides are square.

2 *Retractable steel rule* ideal for measuring long lengths of wood (useful but not essential).

3 *Fretsaw* excellent for cutting around sharp curves.

4 *Coping saw* used for cutting curves.

5 *Mitre saw* an accurate and precise tool useful for sawing mitres, off-cuts or dowel rod.

6 *Tenon saw* for general use.

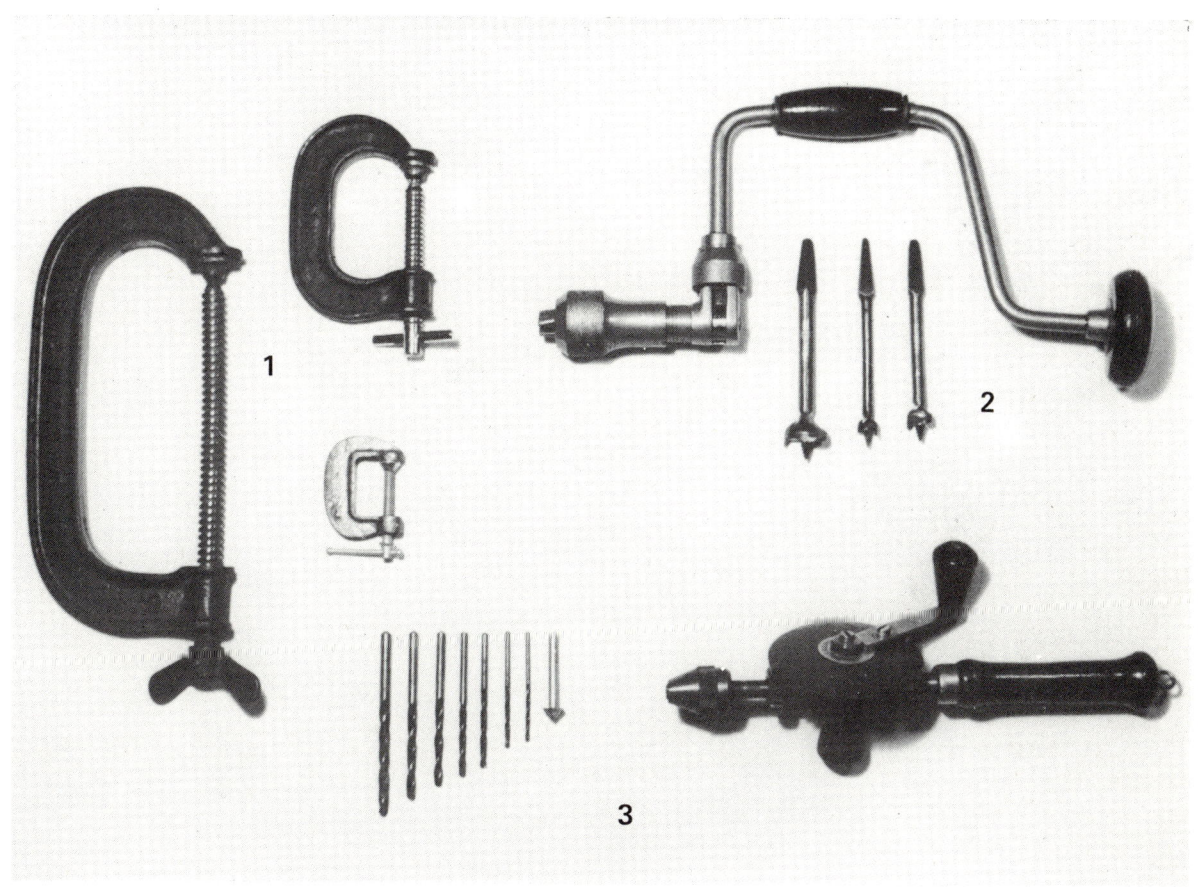

1 *G-clamps* used to secure wood when sawing, and clamping glued wood sections together.
2 *Brace and forstner bits* for drilling large smooth-sided holes.
3 *Hand drill with twist bits and countersink* suitable for general drilling; the countersink is used to inlay screw heads below the wood surface.

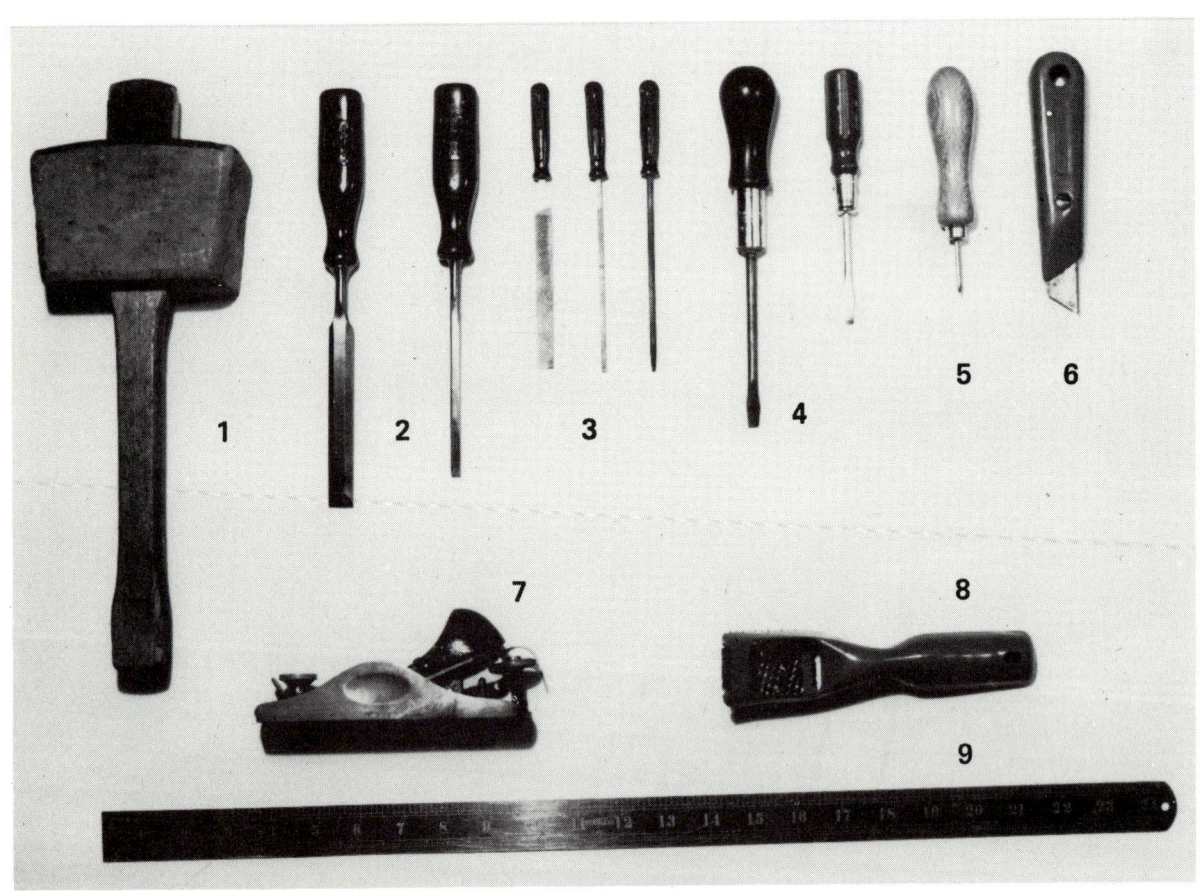

1 *Mallet* for striking chisels (useful but not essential).
2 *Chisels* used for cutting joints, fitting hinges, and shaping wood.
3 *Small files* for intricate shaping (useful but not essential).
4 *Screwdrivers.*
5 *Bradawl* for starting screw holes in softwood.
6 *Stanley knife* for cutting and trimming materials such as veneer and thin plastic.
7 *Jack plane* for smoothing wood and joints (useful but not essential).
8 *Small surform* useful for rounding off corners and sharp edges.
9 *Steel ruler* for accurate measuring and as a straight edge.

Measuring and buying wood

The sizes of wood needed for each project are given in both metric and imperial measurements. Make sure that you use only one system of measuring as the two are not compatible.

With batten, softwood and dowel rod the width is given first, the height second and the length last. Thus for wooden batten 51mm x 25mm x 508mm (2in. x 1in. x 20in.), you must ask your timber merchant for a 508mm (20in.) length of 51mm x 25mm (2in. x 1in.) batten. Usually, the minimum length that a timber merchant will sell is about 305mm (12in.). This means that you have to saw the required length off at home. In this book, the shorter dowel lengths are not specified in the materials lists; few timber merchants would be willing to sell such small quantities (although you could try asking for off-cuts).

With plywood, blockboard and hardboard the thickness is given as the first measurement.

Most batten and softwood that you buy will already be planed smooth. This means that the height and width of the wood will be about 3mm ($\frac{1}{8}$in.) smaller than the size which you specified in the timber-yard. Always check the measurements of your wood before starting a project and make any slight adjustments to the dimensions if necessary.

Different woods

All objects in this book except the parana pine puzzle are made from the types of wood illustrated here. These can be obtained in a wide selection of sizes. The timber merchant will cut your required lengths of wood from the following stock sizes:

Half-round and dowel rod are usually supplied in 182cm (6ft) lengths.
Batten and softwood are supplied in 305cm (10ft) lengths.
Plywood, blockboard and hardboard are supplied in sheets measuring 244cm x 122cm (8ft x 4ft).
Veneer is supplied in sheets of various sizes, and numerous wood grains.

1 Half round rod
2 Dowel rod
3 Batten
4 Softwood
5 Plywood
6 Mahogany plywood
7 Blockboard
8 Hardboard
9 Veneer

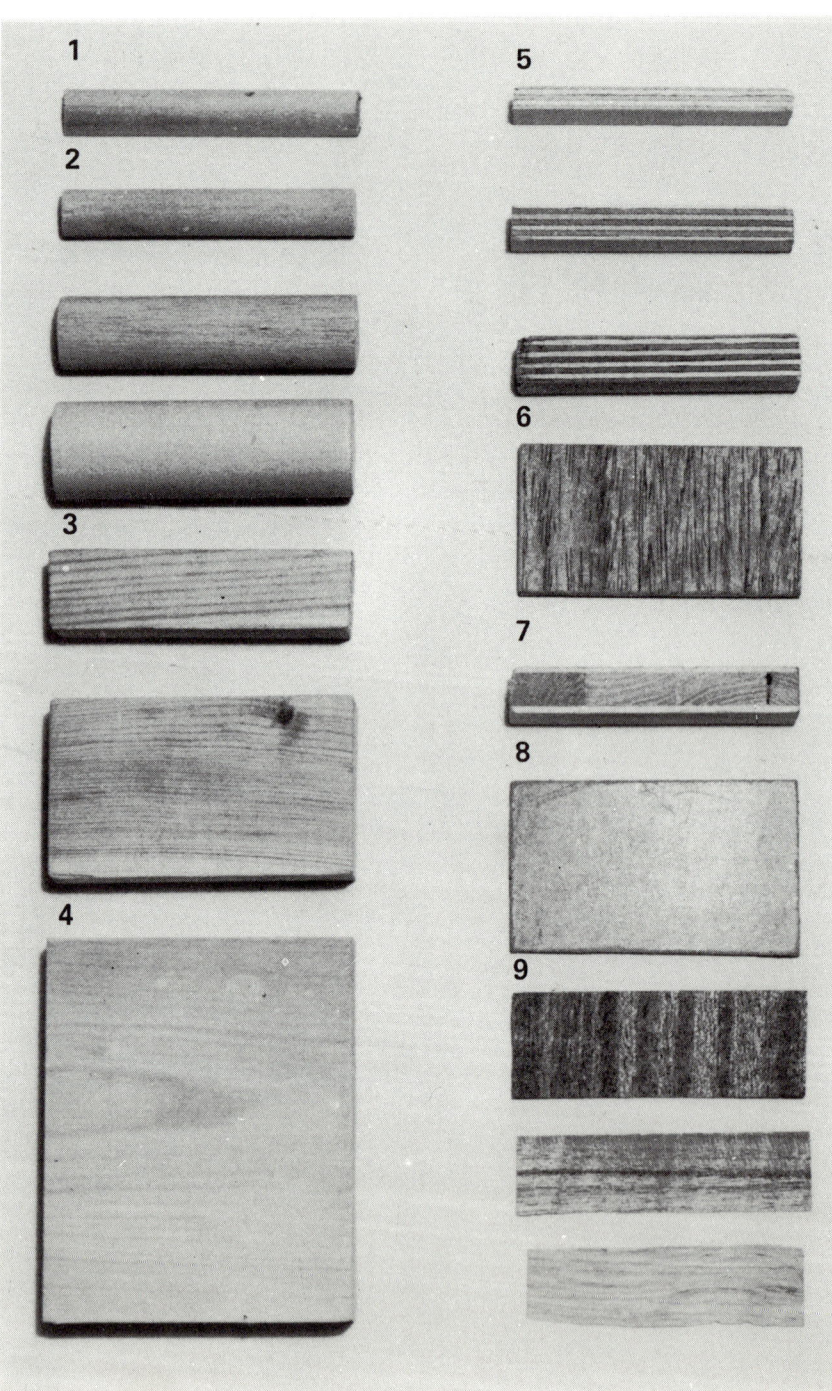

BASIC TECHNIQUES

Sawing

When sawing wood it is very important to have a sturdy work surface such as a workbench or solid table; a shaky surface would probably result in crooked saw lines and a frayed temper.

If you do not have a permanent work area, it is wise to cover the floor with newspaper to help clean up the sawdust later. You should also have a dustpan and brush on hand to prevent sawdust footprints being made across the carpet.

When clamping a piece of wood to the surface, protect it with a small piece of wood under the G-clamp.

To begin sawing get yourself into a well-balanced position. Starting with a shallow cut, slowly saw along the marked lines, gradually changing the angle of the saw to 45° (see figure 1). It always pays to take your time when sawing; cut on the downward stroke only and do not force the saw but let it do the work for you.

Figure 1 Sawing

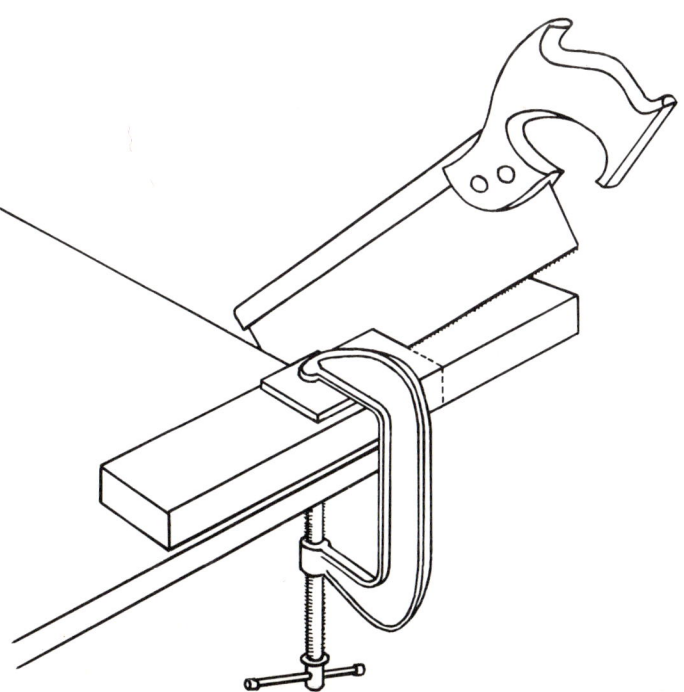

Butt joints

One of the simplest methods of joining two pieces of wood is with a butt joint (figure 2). It is the only kind of joint used in this book. The important point to remember about its construction is that one must be accurate in sawing the right angles; failure to do so will result in a crooked joint. Any gaps in the finished joint can be filled with wood-filler and rubbed down with sandpaper when dry.

Figure 2 Butt joint

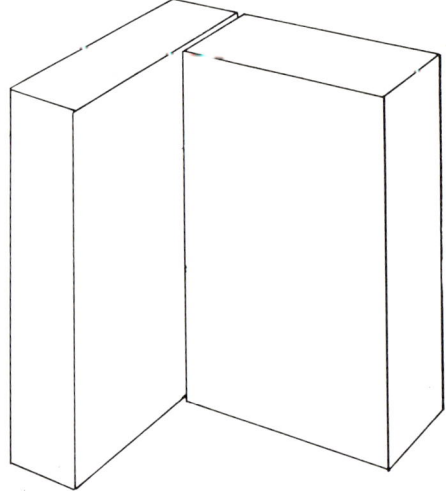

Fitting a hinge

All the hinges used in this book are 30mm (1¼ in.) in length and made of brass. They can be bought, complete with screws, from an ironmongers or a department store. The carved box and large robots will require hinges to be fitted in the following way (figure 3).

Either file down or chisel out a section of the box to the length and depth of the folded hinge. Use a bradawl to start the screw holes. Before screwing the hinge into place, check that the cut out section is flat and smooth, as a bumpy surface will cause the hinge to bend. To fit the hinge to the lid make sure that it is lined up with the middle edge of the lid before screwing, so that when closed it will lay flush with the sides of the box.

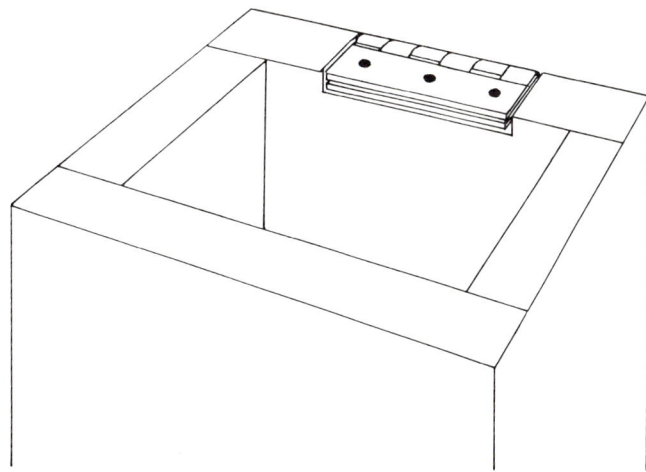

Figure 3 Fitting a hinge

Sawing curves and circles

It is much easier to cut curves and circles with a coping saw or fret-saw, than to struggle with an ordinary one. Both saws serve the same purpose, but the fretsaw uses finer blades and has a much deeper frame, thus giving a greater cutting distance. Spare blades may be bought for both types.

When using these saws, the direction of the blade can easily be changed by turning the handle or adjusting the frame screws.

To cut out an internal shape (figure 4), drill a small hole in the waste area. Remove the saw blade from one end of the saw and push it through the hole. Attach the blade back on the saw frame, and saw using long downward strokes. It pays to be patient while sawing because the blades are brittle and snap easily.

To fit new blades, loosen the handle or frame screws, fit the blade in both slits and tighten.

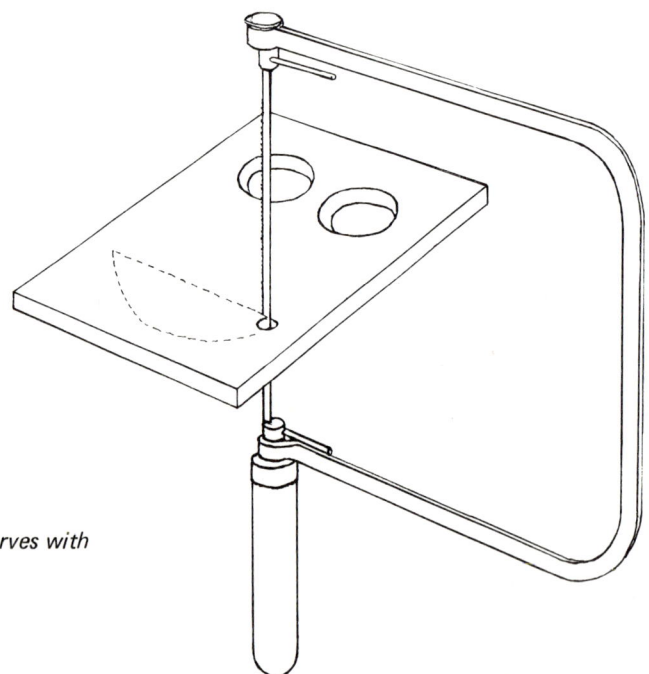

Figure 4 Cutting curves with the coping saw

Making wheels

Dowel rod can be bought from any timber merchant. It is obtainable in a variety of diameters ranging from 3mm (⅛in.) to 51mm (2in.). If the latter is difficult to acquire, a cheap rolling pin is an acceptable substitute. Wheels can also be made from any round wood that would otherwise be thrown away, such as an old broom handle or a broken chair leg.

An easy way to make wheels of even thickness is to wrap masking tape around the dowel, checking that the edges of the tape overlap accurately. Use the tape edge as a guideline when sawing (figure 5).

It is important to be accurate in marking the centre of each wheel, otherwise the toy will wobble along instead of running smoothly. For larger wheels an easy way of marking the centre is to use a paper template with a small central hole. To make one, cut a paper circle the same diameter as the wheel and fold it into eight segments. Cut the point off the narrow end and unfold the paper.

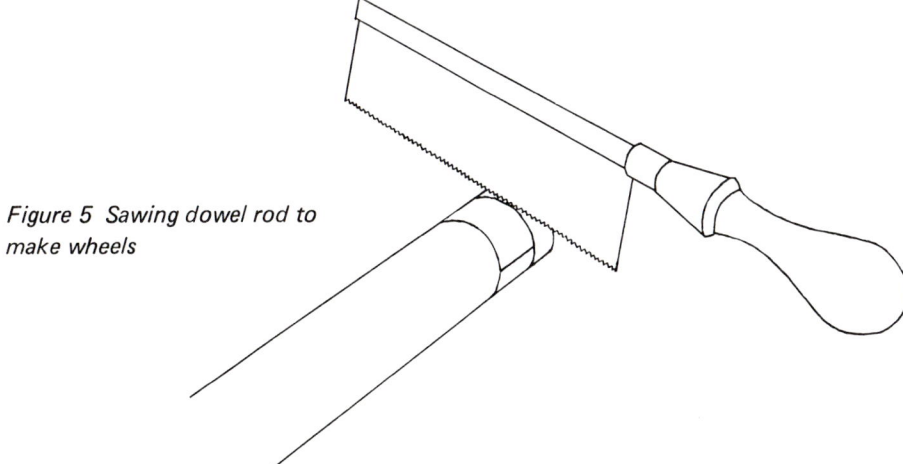

Figure 5 Sawing dowel rod to make wheels

Throughout this book round-headed screws are used to attach the wheels to the toys. Ordinary screws are unsuitable because they have sharp edges which might harm children's fingers.

DECORATING AND FINISHING WOOD

Wood has a natural beauty and texture of its own, but when used to make a much-handled toy it can quickly become dirty. For this reason it is important to smooth all surfaces with sandpaper and apply a protective coat of paint, varnish, polish or bees-wax.

Before applying surface finishes, prepare the wood by removing dirty marks and sharp edges with fine and medium grade sandpaper. Defects such as dents and cracks can be filled with wood-filler and sandpapered when dry.

Paint applied to untreated wood tends to be absorbed into the wood in patches, so it is best to use one coat of wood primer first. When dry, apply one coat of paint. If a really smooth finish is required, rub down with either wet and dry or fine sandpaper and apply a second coat of paint. If several colours are used on one object, an easy method of obtaining crisp straight lines is to use a strip of masking tape to mask off the areas which are not to be painted.

If you wish to apply colour to a toy without obscuring the wood grain, transparent paints are available. At least two coats will need to be applied to achieve any depth of colour.

To enhance the natural wood grain, apply either clear varnish or French polish (shellac), or rub in bees-wax. Wood stains in different shades can also be used effectively to emphasize the natural grain, as well as to give colour to the wood.

Texture and experimental finishes
Most of the toys and puzzles in this book are designed to have smooth surfaces, but you might like to add certain textures, such as a rough stone-like texture on the castle walls. Many interesting finishes can be achieved depending on the tools you have available. It is best to experiment on scrap wood first to find a satisfactory and easy method. Here are a few suggestions which you may like to try.

1

2

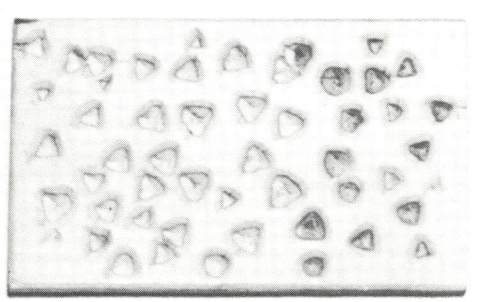

3

4

Plywood   1   *Filed lines, using the plywood lamination as part of the design*
                 2   *Drilled with a stone grinding bit, then stained*
                 3   *Surface indentations, drilled with a large bit*
                 4   *Drilled with a stone grinding bit*

Softwood   5   *Filed lines against the grain*
                 6   *Parts of the surface burnt and rubbed down with a wire brush*
                 7   *Drilled with a countersink, then stained*
                 8   *Parts of the surface chiselled away, then stained*

5

6

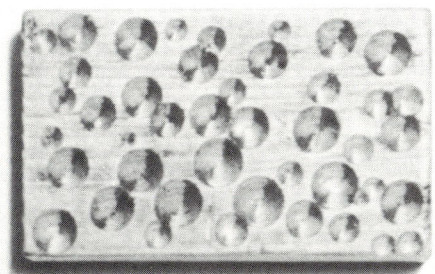

7

8

USEFUL HINTS

1 If your wood is dirty or stained, clean before use with coarse sandpaper. It is much easier to sandpaper separate pieces than an assembled toy.

2 Alway use a try-square when marking right angles; crooked edges look untidy.

3 Secure wood with a G-clamp or vice whenever possible while working; this leaves both hands free and helps to prevent accidents.

4 Never throw wood off-cuts away. Store them in a cardboard box and use them to make other toys.

5 Always give glue adequate time to dry; you do not want your toy to fall apart in your hands.

6 Round off the edges on all toys with fine or medium grade sandpaper, this gives a more professional finish. Always sand in the direction of the grain.

7 To attach screws easily, first drill a small hole to the same depth as the screw length.

8 Read the manufacturers' instructions carefully on tins of paint, varnish and glue before application.

9 When making toys for very young children always use non-toxic paint and varnish; if a paint is not specified as non-toxic it could be poisonous.

10 After using paint or varnish always replace the lid or cap securely, otherwise a skin will form on top of the liquid.

11 After applying paint or varnish, leave the toy to dry in a dust-free place, otherwise particles will adhere to the surface and give it a speckled appearance when dry.

12 Clean paint brushes immediately after use by standing them in a jar of white spirit for a few minutes and wiping with a newspaper and rag: nothing is worse than trying to paint a toy with a stiff caked-up brush.

RACING CARS

Many different shaped cars can be made from a basic rectangle of wooden batten, and four wheels cut from dowel rod and attached with screws. Once completed, each racer can be painted in a different colour, or have a number printed on the side, or a clear polyurethane varnish can be applied to enhance the natural grain of the wood.

Streamlined Racing Car

Tools

Tenon saw, G-clamp or vice, drill with 1mm (1/16in.) and 5mm (3/16in.) bits, screw-driver, small paint brush, ruler, pencil

Materials

Wooden batten, 50mm x 25mm x 178mm (2in. x 1in. x 7in.)
Dowel rod, 38mm (1½in.) diameter
Four 25mm (1in.) round-headed screws
Clear polyurethane varnish
Masking tape
Fine grade sandpaper

To make the racing car

Transfer the measurements in figure 6 to the batten using the ruler and pencil. Secure it with the G-clamp and saw.
Drill four 1mm (1/16in.) holes at the marked points to accommodate the screws.
Sandpaper all over, removing rough and sharp edges.

To make the wheels

Divide the dowel into four 19mm (3/4in.) sections.
Wrap masking tape around the dowel and saw.
Secure each piece in the vice and drill a 5mm (3/16in.) hole through the centre.
Attach the screws loosely so that the wheels can rotate freely.

Finishing

Apply clear polyurethane varnish or paint if desired.

Figure 6 Racing car body measurements

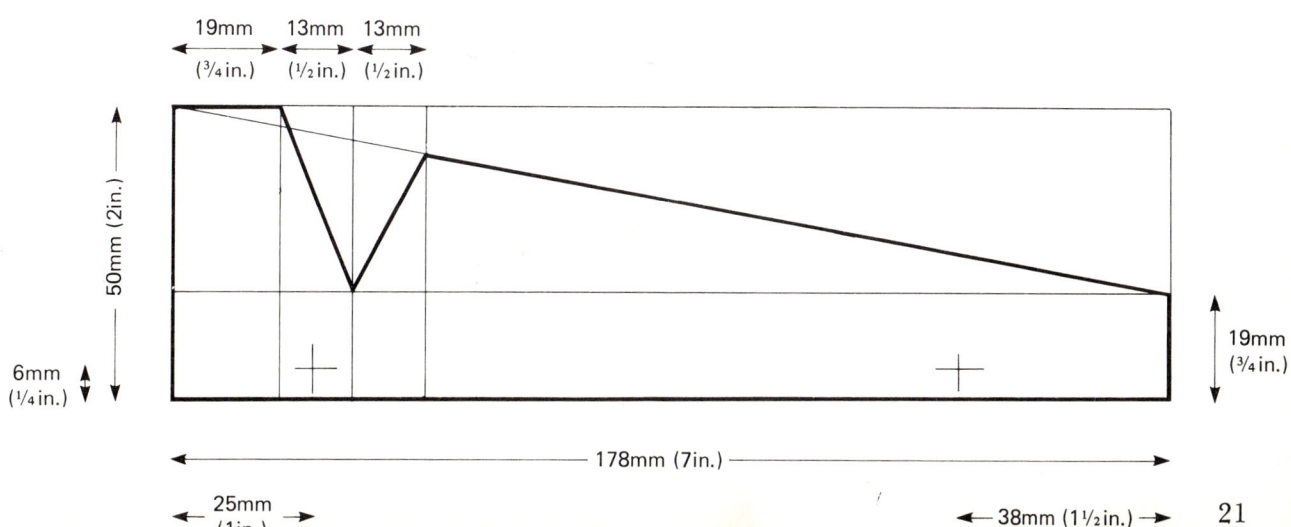

21

Large Racing Car

Tools
Tenon saw, G-clamp or vice, drill with 1mm ($\frac{1}{16}$in.) and 5mm ($\frac{3}{16}$in.) bits, screwdriver, set square, small paint brush, ruler, pencil

Materials
Wooden batten, 51mm x 51mm x 230mm (2in. x 2in. x 9in.)
Dowel rod, 51mm (2in.) diameter
Four 38mm (1$\frac{1}{2}$in.) round-headed screws
Wood glue
Clear polyurethane varnish
Masking tape
Fine and medium grade sandpaper

These chunky racing cars need only a gentle push to send them speeding across the floor. Their wide wheels give them extra stability.

To make the racing car
Secure the batten with the G-clamp and saw off one end at an angle of 45 degrees.
Glue the off-cut on top of the body (see photograph).
Saw off the front of the car at an angle.
On the body, mark four points 6mm ($\frac{1}{4}$in.) up from the base, 51mm (2in.) from the back, and 64mm (2$\frac{1}{2}$in.) from the front: clamp, and drill 1mm ($\frac{1}{16}$in.) holes.
Sandpaper all over, removing all rough and sharp edges.

To make the wheels
Divide the dowel into four 22mm ($\frac{7}{8}$in.) sections.
Wrap masking tape around the dowel and saw.
Secure each piece in the vice and drill a 5mm ($\frac{3}{16}$in.) hole through the centre.
Attach the screws loosely so that the wheels can rotate freely.

Finishing
Apply varnish to enhance the natural grain of the wood.

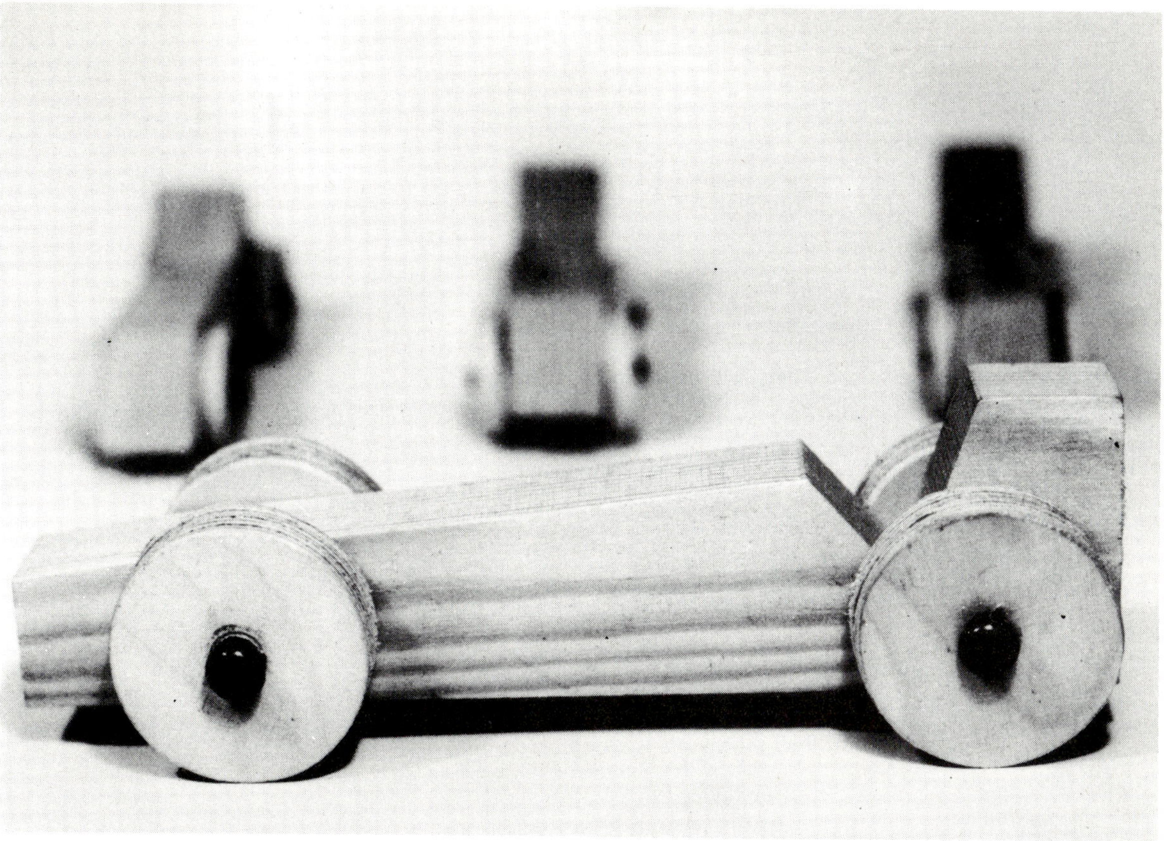

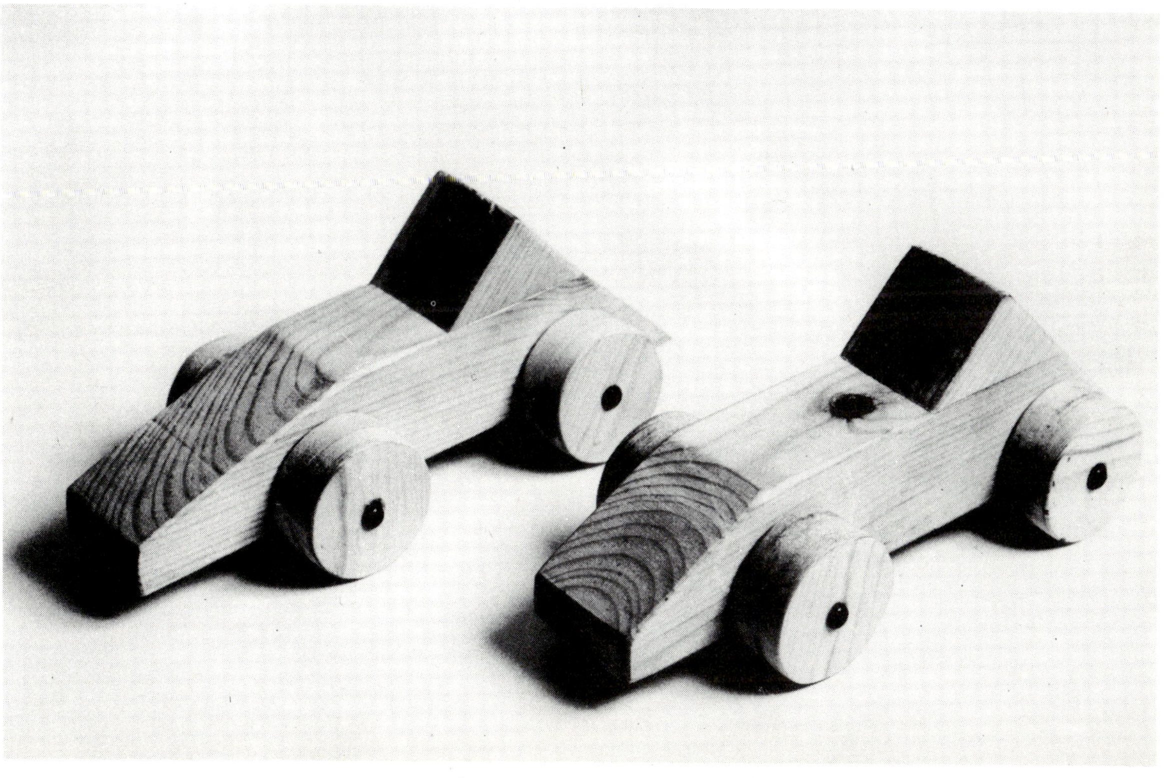

Small Racing Car Set

Tools
Tenon saw, G-clamp or vice, set square, bradawl, small screwdriver, ruler, pencil

Materials
Wooden batten, 25mm x 25mm x 305mm (1in. x 1in. x 12in.)
Dowel rod, 25mm (1in.) diameter
Twelve 19mm (¾in.) round-headed screws
Wood glue
Masking tape
Fine grade sandpaper

These instructions are for a set of three cars of varying shape: to obtain different shaped cars, vary the angles when making the body.

To make the racing cars
Divide the batten into three 102mm (4in.) sections.
Clamp, and saw the end off each piece at an angle.
Glue an off-cut on top of each body (see photograph).
On the bodies mark four points for the wheels 5mm (³/₁₆in.) up from the base, 22mm (⅞in.) from the back and front: start the wheel holes with the bradawl.
Sandpaper all over, removing rough and sharp edges.

To make the wheels
Divide the dowel into twelve 8mm (⁵/₁₆in.) sections.
Wrap masking tape around the dowel, and saw.
Secure each piece in the vice and drill a 3mm (⅛in.) hole through the centre.
Attach the screws loosely so that the wheels can rotate freely.

Robot family

Pencil and ruler box

*Small racing cars, length
102mm (4in.)*

APPLE JIGSAW

Tools
Tenon saw, coping saw,
G-clamp, small paint brush,
ruler, pencil

Materials
Plywood, 3mm (⅛in.) thick,
610mm x 305mm (24in. x
12in.)
Non-toxic green and red paint
Clear non-toxic varnish
White spirit
Fine grade sandpaper
Impact adhesive (such as
Evostik)

This attractive jigsaw could also be hung on a wall and used as a
decorative panel. After making the apple, invent some fruit puzzles
of your own.

To make the jigsaw
Divide the plywood into two pieces both measuring 305mm x 305mm
(12in. x 12in.).
Secure with the clamp and saw.
Work out the apple design on paper using curved lines.
Transfer the design to one piece of plywood using the pencil.
Secure with the clamp and saw into sections.
Mount the surround on the other piece of plywood using *Evostik,*
following the instructions on the can.
Sandpaper all the pieces and the surround.

Finishing
Paint the apple red and green.
Paint the stalk brown using the red and green paint mixed together.
Apply varnish to all pieces, including the surround.

Apple jigsaw, 305mm x
305mm (12in. x 12in.)

FOUR-PIECE PUZZLE

Tools
Tenon saw, G-clamp, small paint brush, ruler, pencil

Materials
Softwood, 13mm (½in.) thick, 95mm x 95mm (3¾in. x 3¾in.)
Medium grade sandpaper
Clear non-toxic varnish

Simple to make and easy to put together, this could be a young child's first puzzle. As an alternative, stick a coloured illustration from a magazine on one side of the wood before varnishing.

To make the puzzle
Transfer the measurements in figure 7 to the piece of wood using the ruler and pencil.
Secure the wood with the G-clamp and saw into sections.
Sandpaper each piece removing all sharp edges.

Finishing
Apply clear varnish to enhance the grain of the wood.

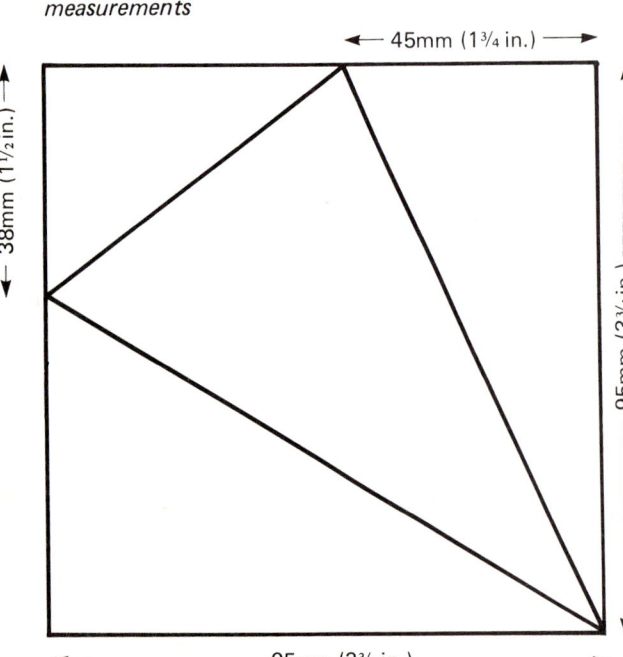

Figure 7 Four-piece puzzle measurements

45mm (1¾ in.)

38mm (1½ in.)

95mm (3¾ in.)

95mm (3¾ in.)

Four-piece puzzle, 95mm x 95mm (3¾in. x 3¾in.)

WOODEN COLLAGE

Tools

Tenon saw, coping saw, G-clamp or vice, 3mm (⅛in.) chisel, Stanley knife, ruler, pencil

Materials

Plywood, 3mm (⅛in.) thick, 305mm x 165mm (12in. x 6½in.)
Small sticks (such as flower canes)
Wooden off-cuts
Wood glue
Clear polyurethane varnish
Fine and medium grade sandpaper

Wooden shapes can be cut out and glued onto a base board to form a collage or wall picture. Alternatively, the shapes can be used as 'two-dimensional' toys, to be moved around and played with on a flat surface. If you are not satisfied with just one house, why not make a whole street of buildings from shops to cinemas, using this wooden collage technique.

To make the house collage

Mark, clamp and saw two pieces of plywood: the base measuring 165mm x 165mm (6½in. x 6½in.) and one piece measuring 165mm x 57mm (6½in. x 2¼in.).
Glue the smaller piece on top of one end of the base: draw in the shape of the roof and chimney, clamp and saw along the marked lines.

Wooden collage, 165mm x 165mm (6½in. x 6½in.)

Glue off-cuts into place for the windows and door.
Cover the remainder of the house with sticks using the Stanley knife
to cut the required lengths, and glue into place.

To make the tree and sun
Draw a tree shape on the remainder of the plywood and cut out using
the coping saw.
Clamp, and split parts of the top layer of ply with the chisel to
achieve a two-tone effect.
Use a dowel off-cut for the sun, or cut out a circle using the coping
saw.

Finishing
Apply clear varnish to all parts.

Van, length 178mm (7in.)

VAN

Tools
Tenon saw, G-clamp or vice, drill with 3mm (⅛ in.) bit, try-square, bradawl, small paint brush, ruler, pencil

Materials
Softwood, 82mm x 38mm x 178mm (3¼ in. x 1½ in. x 7in.)
Dowel rod, 38mm (1½ in.) diameter
Four 25mm (1in.) round-headed screws
Dark wood stain
Medium and fine grade sandpaper
Masking tape

This easy-to-make van requires little sawing. For an alternative finish apply red transparent polyurethane varnish.

To make the van
Transfer the measurements in figure 8 to the piece of wood using the try-square, ruler and pencil: secure with the G-clamp and saw.
Sandpaper, rounding off all sharp edges.
Mark in the position of the wheels (figure 8): start the screw holes with the bradawl.

To make the wheels
Divide the dowel into four 10mm (⅜ in.) sections.
Wrap masking tape around the dowel and saw.
Secure each piece in the vice and drill a 3mm (⅛ in.) hole through the centre.
Attach the screws loosely so that the wheels can rotate freely.

Finishing
Apply dark wood stain.

Figure 8 Van body measurements

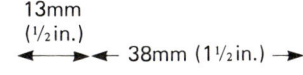

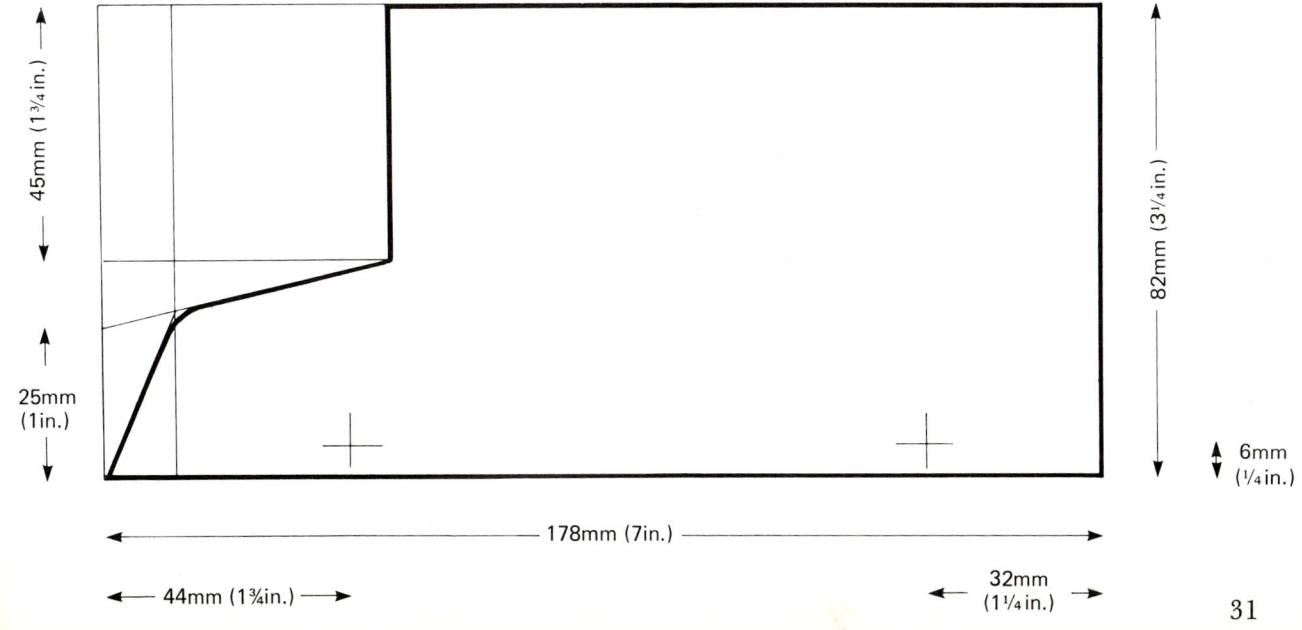

SKITTLES

Round Skittles

Tools
Tenon saw, G-clamp or vice, small paint brush, ruler, pencil

Materials
Dowel rod, 25mm (1in.) diameter, 1500mm (60in.)
Paint or clear polyurethane varnish
Fine grade sandpaper
Masking tape

These simple skittles are easy to make and great fun to play with. They can even be made from an old broom handle.

To make the skittles
Divide the dowel into ten 150mm (6in.) sections.
To obtain a right-angled edge, wrap masking tape around the marked points; the edges of the tape should overlap accurately as this is your sawing guideline.
Secure the dowel in the vice and saw into sections.
Make sure that each skittle stands upright: any slight imbalance should be corrected with sandpaper or a file.
Sandpaper each piece removing all sharp edges.

Finishing
Varnish or paint as desired.

The ball
A light plastic ball can be used to knock down the skittles or wooden balls may be obtained from a shop listed in the back of this book.

Round skittles, height 150mm (6in.)

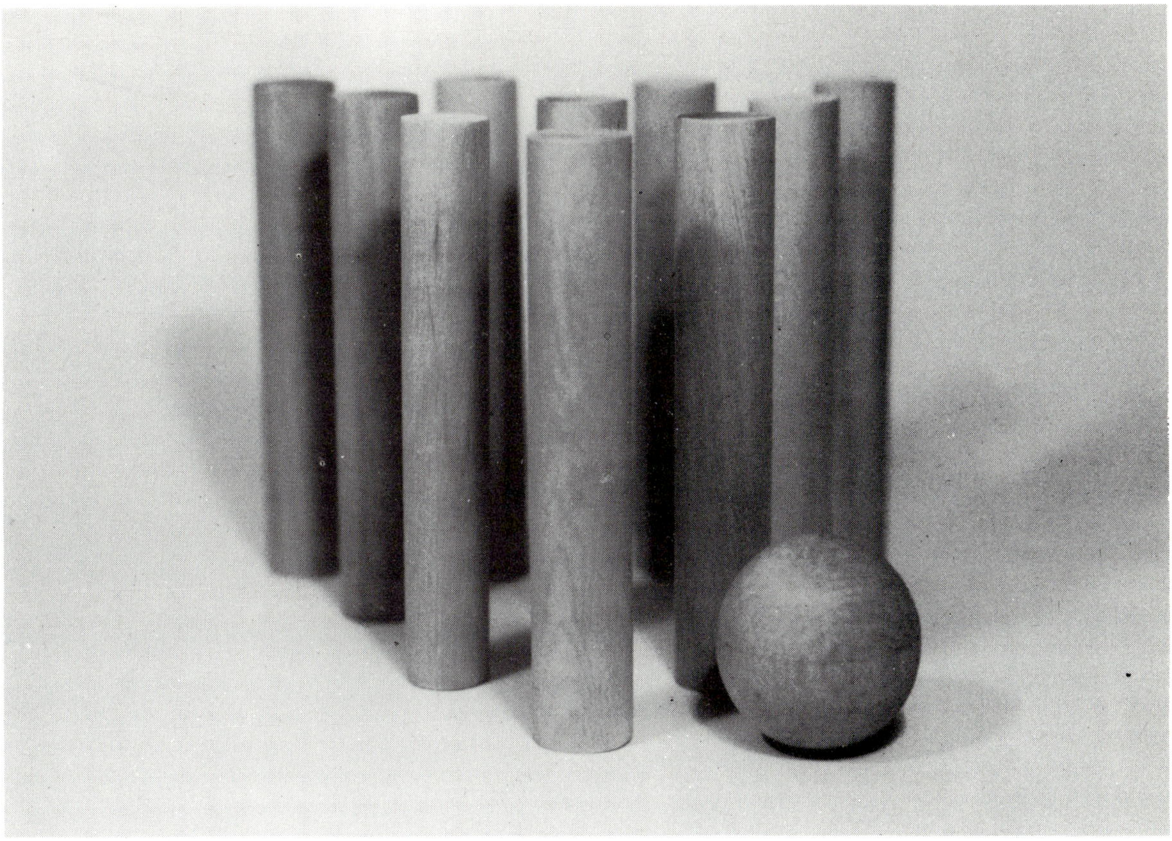

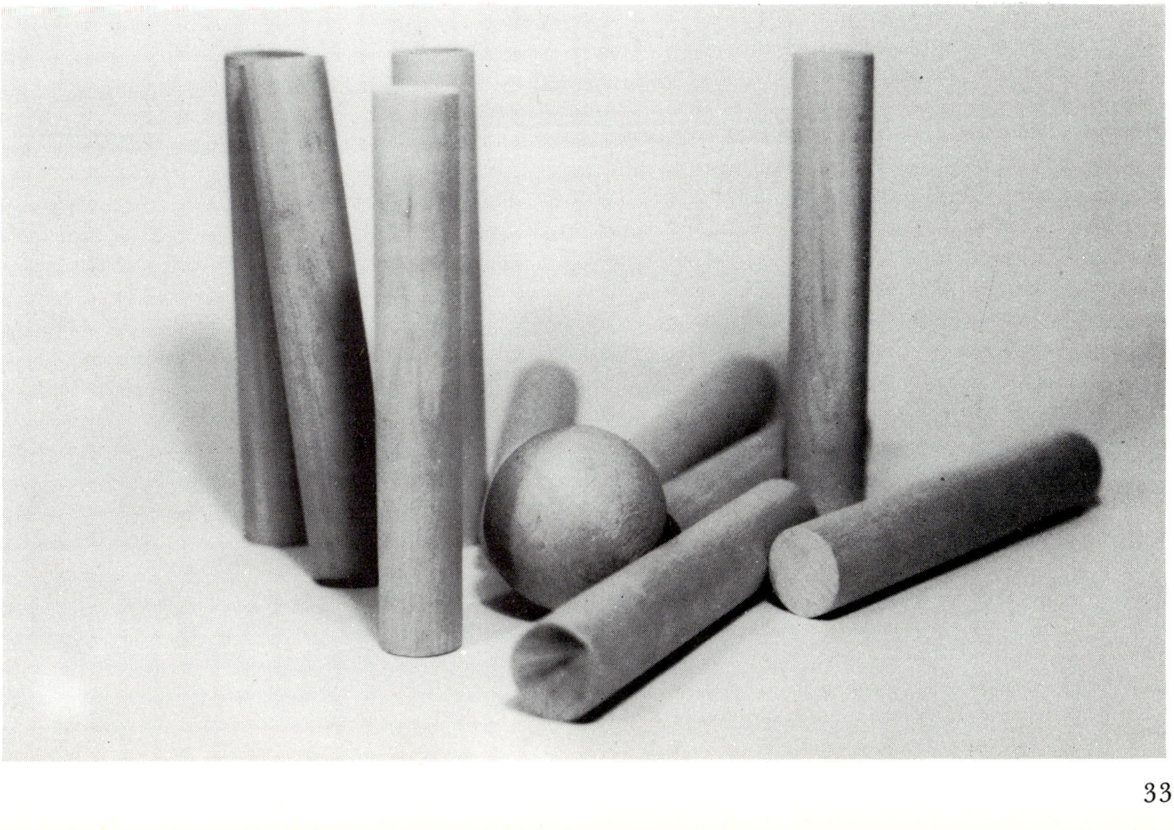

Square Skittles

Tools

Tenon saw, G-clamp or vice, try-square, small paint brush, ruler, pencil

Materials

Wooden batten, 25mm x 25mm x 1500mm (1in. x 1in. x 60in.)
Paint or clear polyurethane varnish
Fine grade sandpaper

To make the skittles

Divide the batten into ten 150mm (6in.) sections.

Mark three sides of the wood at each division using the try-square: when sawing keep to the marked lines to obtain an accurate right angle.

Secure the batten with the G-clamp and saw the length into sections. Make sure that each skittle stands upright: any slight imbalance should be corrected with sandpaper or a file.

Sandpaper each piece removing all sharp edges.

Finishing

Varnish or paint as desired.

The ball

A light plastic ball can be used to knock down the skittles, or wooden balls may be obtained from a shop listed in the back of this book.

Square skittles, height 150mm (6in.)

CIRCULAR PUZZLE

Tools
Coping saw, tenon saw, chisels 3mm (⅛in.) and 6mm (¼in.), compass, G-clamp, small paint brush, ruler, pencil

Materials
Plywood, 9mm (⅜in.) thick, 230mm x 230mm (9in. x 9in.)
Dark wood stain
Paper

The unusual texture of this puzzle is achieved by splitting the top lamination of the wood. It makes the puzzle difficult for the participant to piece together, as there is no continous woodgrain to give him clues.

To make the puzzle
Draw a circle 230mm (9in.) in diameter on the wood.
Work out a design on paper using straight lines.
Draw the design on to the wood using the ruler and pencil.
Cut out the circle using the coping saw.
Saw the circle into sections using the tenon saw.
Secure each piece with the clamp or in a vice and, using the chisel, split the top layer of ply on each piece to achieve a two-tone effect: take only part of the top layer away.

Finishing
Apply a dark wood stain.

*Circular puzzle, 229mm
(9in.) diameter*

HOOP-LA

Tools

Coping saw, G-clamp, brace with 19mm (3/4 in.) bit, drill with 3mm (1/8 in.) bit, small paint brush, compass, ruler, pencil

Materials

Plywood, 3mm (1/8 in.) thick, 380mm x 380mm (15in. x 15in.)
Dowel rod, 19mm (3/4 in.) diameter, 305mm (12in.)
Gloss paint in five different colours
Wood-filler
Wood primer
Wood glue
Fine and medium grade sandpaper

Children will have fun trying to throw these hoops over the stick. Make an outdoor version to stick into the ground by sharpening the dowel to a point before pushing through the base.

To make the hoops

Divide the plywood into four equal squares.
Centre the compass in each square and draw two circles 89mm (3½ in.) and 29mm (1⅛ in.) radius.
Secure the plywood with the clamp and drill a hole just inside the circumference of each inner circle: insert the coping saw and cut out the inner and outer circles.
Glue the inner circle off-cuts together to form the base: when dry fill any visible drill holes with wood-filler.
Secure the base with the clamp and drill a 19mm (3/4 in.) hole through the centre.
Push the dowel into the base, using wood glue if it is loose.
Sandpaper each piece removing all sharp edges.

Finishing

Apply wood primer to all pieces: when dry paint with various colours.

Hoop-la, height 305mm (12in.)

BUILDING BLOCKS

Tools
Tenon saw, G-clamp, small paint brush, ruler, pencil

Materials
40 wooden off-cuts of varying size and shape
Fine and medium grade sandpaper
Paint or clear varnish (non-toxic)

An excellent way of using up all your off-cuts and left-over lengths of wood, this project involves little sawing as the majority of the pieces are already made.

To make the blocks
If any of the off-cuts are too large, secure with the G-clamp and saw to a manageable size.
Sandpaper each block, removing all rough and sharp edges.

Finishing
Varnish or paint with a variety of bright colours.

Building blocks

CONSTRUCTION KIT

Tools
Tenon saw, G-clamp or vice, drill with 6mm (¼in.) bit, small paint brush, ruler, pencil

Materials
30 wooden off-cuts of varying size and shape
Dowel rod, 6mm (¼in.) diameter, 610mm (24in.)
Fine and medium grade sandpaper
Clear non-toxic varnish

Another way of using up off-cuts is to make an interchangeable construction kit using dowel rod to link the pieces.

To make the blocks
If any off-cuts are too large, secure with the G-clamp and saw to a manageable size.
Secure each off-cut in the vice and drill a 6mm (¼in.) hole: drill several holes in the larger blocks.
Saw the dowel into various lengths.
Sandpaper the blocks and dowel, removing all rough and sharp edges.

Finishing
Apply a clear non-toxic varnish.

LORRY

Tools
Tenon saw, G-clamp, drill with 5mm ($\frac{3}{16}$in.) and 2mm ($\frac{1}{16}$in.) bits, try-square, screwdriver, small paint brush, ruler, pencil

Materials
Softwood, 76mm x 51mm x 325mm (3in. x 2in. x 12$\frac{3}{4}$in.)
Dowel rod, 51mm (2in.) diameter
Four 25mm (1in.) round-headed screws
Clear polyurethane varnish
Wood glue
Masking tape
Fine and medium grade sandpaper

A solid and robust toy, this lorry will stand up to the roughest handling. When choosing your wood, look for a piece with an attractive grain.

To make the lorry
Divide the softwood into two pieces, 133mm (5$\frac{1}{4}$in.) and 190 mm (7$\frac{1}{2}$in.) in length.
Mark three sides of the wood at each division using the try-square: when sawing, keep to the lines to obtain an accurate right angle.
Transfer the measurements in figure 9 onto the wood using the ruler and pencil: secure with the G-clamp and saw.
Sandpaper both parts of the lorry removing all sharp edges.
Glue the 133mm (5$\frac{1}{4}$in.) block onto the body.
Drill four 2mm ($\frac{1}{16}$in.) holes at the marked points to accommodate the screws.

To make the wheels
Divide the dowel into four 10mm ($\frac{3}{8}$in.) sections.
Wrap masking tape around the dowel, clamp and saw.
Secure with the G-clamp and drill a 5mm ($\frac{3}{16}$in.) hole through the centre of each wheel.
Attach the screws loosely so that the wheels can rotate freely.

Finishing
Apply clear polyurethane varnish to enhance the natural grain of the wood.

*Figure 9 Lorry body
measurements*

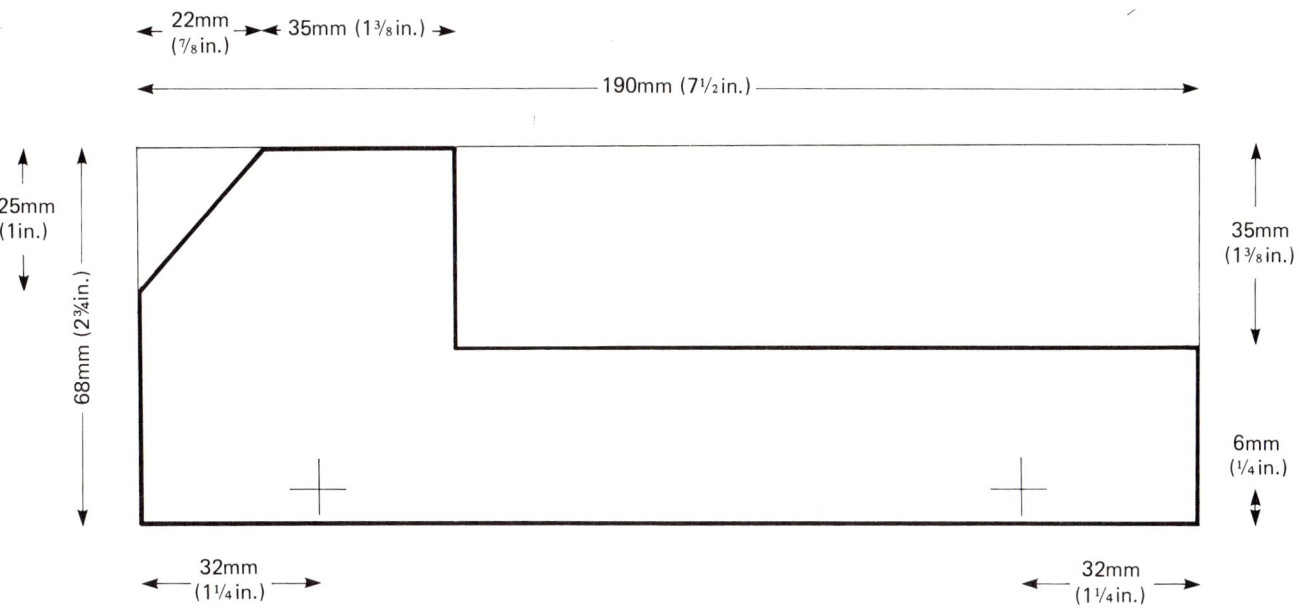

Lorry, length 190mm (7½in.)

NOUGHTS AND CROSSES

Small Noughts and Crosses

Tools
Tenon saw, G-clamp or vice, try-square, ruler, pencil

Materials
Mahogany plywood, 3mm (1/8 in.) thick, 145 mm x 145 mm (5 3/4 in. x 5 3/4 in.)
Plywood, 10mm (3/8 in.) thick, 76mm x 145mm (3in. x 5 3/4 in.)
Dowel rod, 13mm (1/2 in.) diameter
Wood glue
Clear polyurethane varnish
Masking tape
Fine and medium grade sandpaper

This is a pocket sized noughts and crosses board, ideal for keeping children amused on long journeys. For a professional finish, a square of felt could be glued underneath the board.

To make the board
Measure and mark two points 45mm (1 3/4 in.) from each corner of the mahogany plywood and join them with a line to form a cross.
Divide the 10mm (3/8 in.) plywood into four 6mm (1/4 in.) wide strips; clamp and saw into sections.
Divide two of the strips into six pieces measuring 45mm (1 3/4 in.); clamp and saw.
Sandpaper the board and divisions removing all sharp edges.
Glue the divisions onto the board keeping to the inside of the drawn lines.

To make the noughts and crosses
Using the pencil, mark a 19mm (3/4 in.) wide strip of plywood and divide it into five 19mm (3/4 in.) sections.
Mark a 6mm (1/4 in.) square in each corner of every section: clamp or secure in the vice and cut out the crosses.
Divide the 13mm (1/2 in.) dowel into five 13mm (1/2 in.) sections.
Wrap masking tape around the dowel, clamp and saw.
Sandpaper the noughts and crosses removing all sharp edges.

Finishing
Apply clear varnish to the board.

Small noughts and crosses, 145mm x 145mm (5¾in. x 5¾in.)

Large Noughts and Crosses

Tools
Tenon saw, G-clamp or vice, try-square, ruler, pencil

Materials
Blockboard, 13mm (½in.) thick, 305mm x 305mm (12in. x 12in.)
Wooden batten, 25mm x 25mm x 1220mm (1in. x 1in. x 48in.)
Dowel rod, 38mm (1½in.) diameter, 254mm (10in.)
Softwood, 51mm x 51mm x 254mm (2in. x 2in. x 10in.)
Light and dark wood stain
Wood glue
Masking tape
Fine and medium grade sandpaper

This is a larger version of the noughts and crosses game, played with chunky, three-dimensional pieces.

To make the board
Transfer the measurements in figure 10a to the batten using the try-square, ruler and pencil: clamp and saw into sections.
Sandpaper the board and sections removing all sharp edges.
Glue the sections to the blockboard (figure 10a).

To make the noughts and crosses
Using the try-square, mark three sides of the softwood at five 51mm (2in.) intervals; clamp and saw along the lines to obtain a right-angled edge.
Mark the shape of the cross on each section (figures 10b and 10c), continuing the lines down each side. Clamp and saw, keeping to the drawn lines to obtain right-angled edges.
Divide the dowel into five 51mm (2in.) sections.
Wrap masking tape around the dowel: clamp and saw.

Sandpaper the noughts and crosses removing all sharp edges.

Finishing
Apply a light wood stain to the board and a dark wood stain to the pieces.

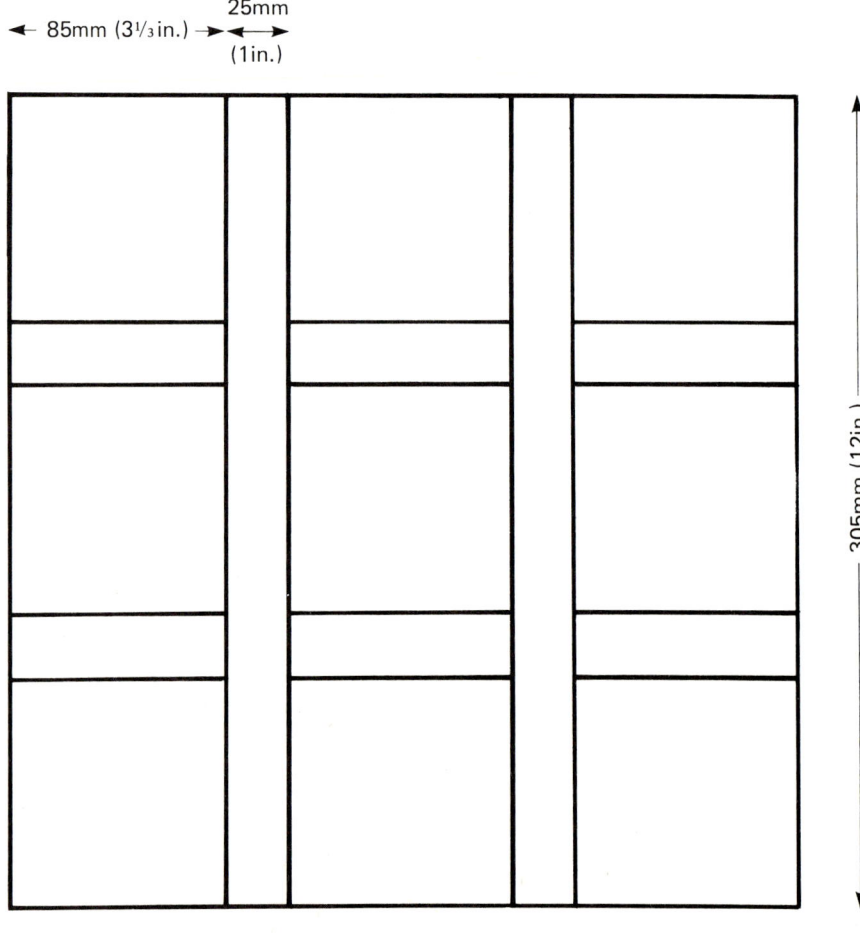

Figure 10a Measurements for the noughts and crosses board

Wooden collage

Apple jigsaw

British Isles map

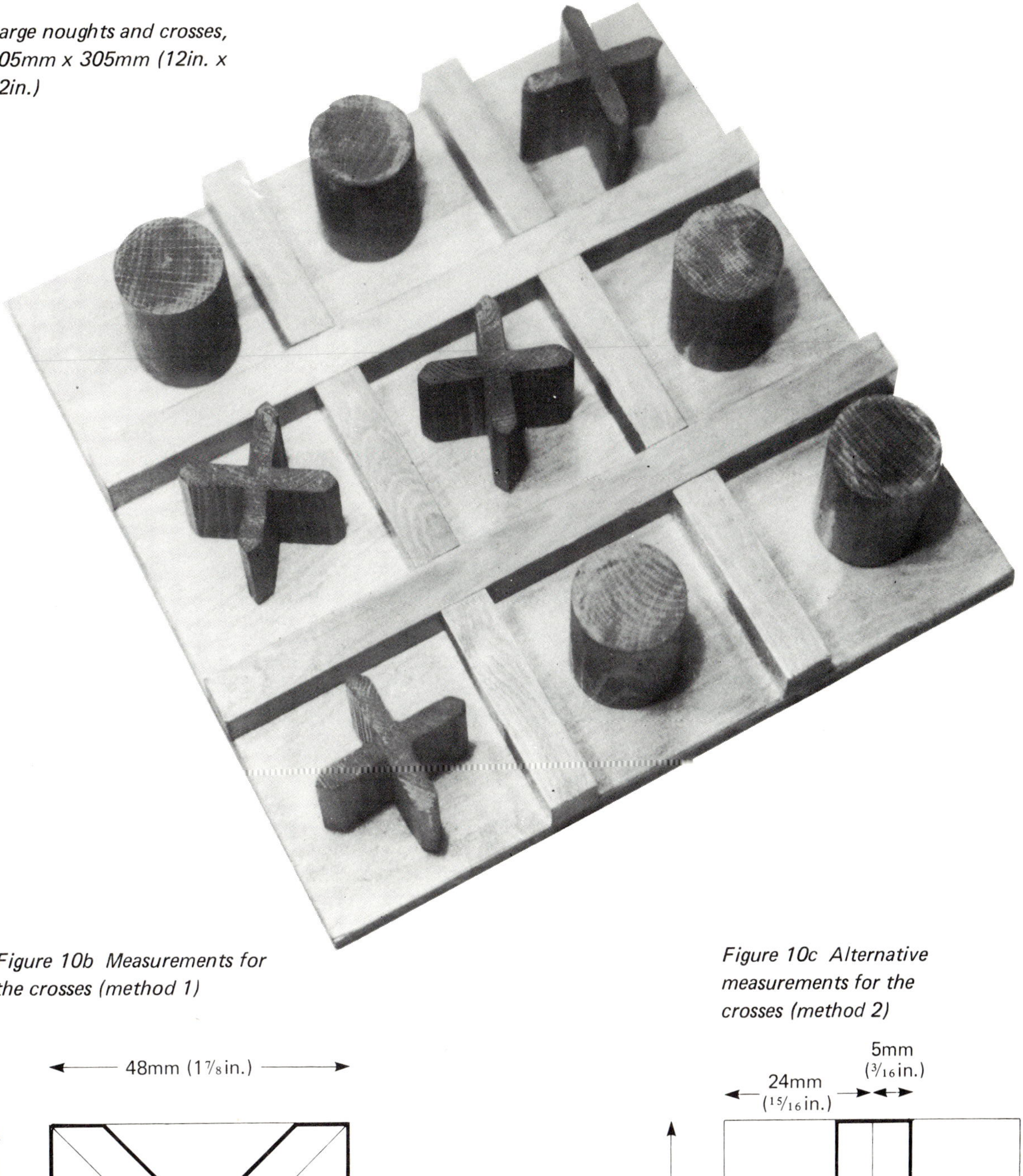

*Large noughts and crosses,
305mm x 305mm (12in. x
12in.)*

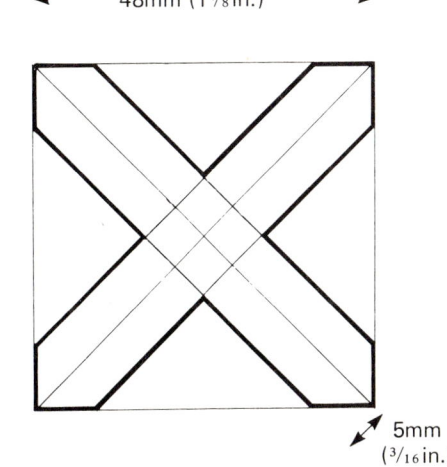

*Figure 10b Measurements for
the crosses (method 1)*

48mm (1⅞in.)

48mm (1⅞in.)

5mm
(³/₁₆in.)

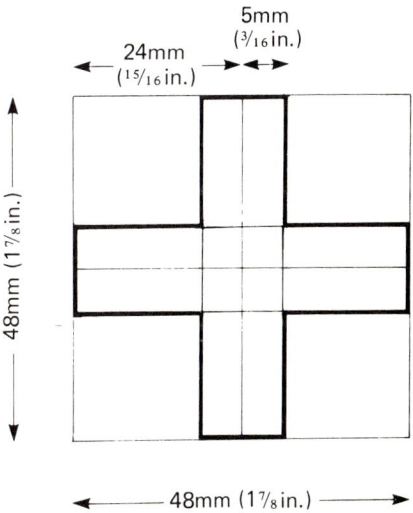

*Figure 10c Alternative
measurements for the
crosses (method 2)*

5mm
(³/₁₆in.)

24mm
(¹⁵/₁₆in.)

48mm (1⅞in.)

48mm (1⅞in.)

49

MONEY-BOXES

Face Money-Box

Tools
Tenon saw, coping saw, G-clamp or vice, try-square, drill with 3mm (1/8 in.) bit, compass, ruler, pencil

Materials
Plywood, 10mm (3/8 in.) thick, 280mm x 190mm (11in. x 7½in.)
Clear perspex, 3mm (1/8 in.) thick, 82mm x 82mm (3¼in. x 3¼in.) or recycled clear plastic from old packaging
Two 25mm (1in.) diameter teddy-bear eyes or transparent coloured buttons
Clear plastic glue (such as *Bostik*)
Wood glue
Clear polyurethane varnish
Find and medium grade sandpaper

A young child will find it great fun to save pennies in this amusing money-box. Teddy-bear eyes are available from department stores or haberdasheries. See-through perspex for the mouth and eyes may be obtained from hardware or do-it-yourself shops, or suppliers listed in the back of this book.

To make the money box
Divide the plywood into the following sizes using the try-square, ruler and pencil: back and front 140mm x 102mm (5½in. x 4 in.); two sides 140mm x 45mm (5½in. x 1¾in); top and bottom 82mm x 45mm (3¼in. x 1¾in.).
Clamp the plywood, and saw into sections.
Using the compass, draw the eye and mouth shapes onto the front piece. Clamp, and drill a 3mm (1/8 in.) hole just inside the eyes and mouth; attach the coping saw and cut out.
Apply wood glue to the edges of the sides, and construct the box shape using butt joints. Clamp or secure the box in the vice, allowing time to dry.
Remove all rough and sharp edges using medium sandpaper.
Clamp the perspex and cut in half with the tenon saw. Using the clear plastic glue, stick the pieces inside the box, covering the eye and mouth holes.
Mark the money-hole on top of the box, measuring 38mm x 13mm (1½in. x ½in.). Drill a 3mm (1/8 in.) hole, and cut out using the coping saw.
Glue the top, the bottom and the nose into place.
Saw the backs off the eyes if necessary, and stick them in place with the clear plastic glue.
Make two ears from the remaining plywood, or use a dowel off-cut sawn in half, and attach these to the sides with wood glue.
Sandpaper all over, using fine grade sandpaper.

Finishing
Apply varnish over all the wood.

Face money-box, height 140mm (5½in.)

Money-Box Sculpture

Tools
Tenon saw, G-clamp or vice, try-square, small paint brush, ruler, pencil

Materials
Plywood, 10mm (³⁄₈in.) thick, 152mm x 381mm (6in. x 15in.)
Wooden off-cuts of varying shape and size
Wooden balls (optional)
Clear polyurethane varnish
Wood glue
Fine and medium grade sandpaper

This is an exciting and unusual money-box which is easier to make than it looks; it is simply an ordinary box with off-cuts glued on the outside.

To make the money-box
Divide the plywood into the following sizes using the try-square, ruler and pencil: back and front 152mm x 102mm (6in. x 4in.), two sides 152mm x 45mm (6in. x 1³⁄₄in.), bottom 102mm x 64mm (4in. x 2¹⁄₂in.). Clamp and saw into sections.
Apply wood glue to the edges of the sides and construct the box shape using butt joints.
Clamp, or secure the box in the vice, allowing the glue time to dry.
Glue the off-cuts to the box concentrating on one side at a time.
Cover the top with off-cuts leaving a slit of 51mm x 13mm (2in. x ¹⁄₂in.) for the money-hole.

Finishing
Apply varnish, completely covering the box.

Sculpture money-box, height
165mm (6½in.)

DOMINOES

Tools

Tenon saw, G-clamp or vice, drill with 3mm ($\frac{1}{8}$in.) bit, try-square, small paint brush, ruler and pencil

Materials

Wooden batten, 51mm x 25mm x 305mm (2in. x 1in. x 12in.)
Medium and fine grade sandpaper
Masking tape
Gloss polyurethane varnish

To make the dominoes

Divide the batten into 28 sections, each 10mm ($\frac{3}{8}$in.) thick.

With a pencil, mark three sides of the wood at each division using the try-square.

Secure the batten with the G-clamp and saw the lengths into sections; keep to the marked lines to obtain a right-angled edge.

Divide each piece in half with a pencil, clamp and run the saw along the pencil line to a depth of 1mm ($\frac{1}{32}$in.).

Mark out the positions of the pips on each piece with a pencil. (Each domino bears a different combination of numbers from blank to six.)

Clamp, and at each marked point drill down to a depth of 2mm ($\frac{1}{16}$in.).

To obtain a consistent depth of indentation wrap masking tape around the drill bit 2mm ($\frac{1}{16}$in.) up from the bottom.

Sandpaper each piece removing all sharp edges.

Finishing

Apply clear gloss varnish to each domino.

If desired, apply wood primer and a coat of coloured paint to the flat side of each domino; this will ensure that players cannot cheat by memorising the wood grain on the backs of certain tiles!

Dominoes

CARVED BOX

Tools

Tenon saw, G-clamp or vice, try-square, round surform or large round file, small screwdriver, bradawl, ruler, pencil, small paint brush, chisel

Materials

Plywood, 10mm (3/8 in.) thick, 305mm x 203mm (12in. x 8in.)
Brass hinge with screws, 25mm (1in.)
Brass hook with eyelet
Wood stain
Masking tape
Fine and medium grade sandpaper

This box can be used to store sweets, jewellery, cigars or a host of other things. When shaping the sides, take care not to carve too much wood away, or gaps will appear.

To make the box

Divide the plywood into the following sizes using the try-square, ruler and pencil: back, front and two sides 76mm x 76mm (3in. x 3in.); top and bottom 76mm x 95mm (3in. x 3¾ in.).
Clamp the plywood and saw into sections.
Apply wood glue to the edges of the sides and construct the box using butt joints. Clamp or secure the box in the vice, and when dry, glue the bottom into place.
To attach the hinge see figure 3 (page 15).
Clamp the box to the edge of the bench or in the vice, and carve diagonally downwards using the surform or file.
When shaping the lid and the top of the box, secure it with masking tape to prevent any movement of the lid.
Sandpaper the box completely.

Finishing

Apply wood stain all over the box.
Screw the hook into the centre-front edge of the lid.
Screw the eyelet into place so that the hook swings through the eyelet.

Carved box, height 95mm (3¾in.)

ADHESIVE BLOCKS

Tools
Tenon saw, G-clamp or vice, screwdriver, drill with 3mm (1/8in.) bit, countersink, scissors, small paint brush, ruler, pencil

Materials
50 wooden off-cuts of varying size and shape
Softwood 102mm x 102mm x 152mm (4in. x 4in. x 6in.)
Mild steel or aluminium bar, 3mm (1/8in.) thick, 19mm x 457mm (3/4in. x 18in.)
Touch fastening strip (such as *Velcro*) 25mm x 1015mm (1in. x 40in.)
Two 25mm (1in.) wood screws
Impact adhesive (such as *Evostik*)
Masking tape
Wood primer
Gloss paint in different colours
Fine and medium grade sandpaper

The irregularly-shaped blocks on the stem of this sculptural toy can quickly be rearranged in any order. They each have a touch fastening strip glued to the back, so all you have to do is pull the pieces off, and the backing will instantly adhere in any new position. *Velcro* is a fastener which consists of two tapes, one of which has a fluffy surface, the other of which has tiny plastic hooks; where they touch they fasten instantly. *Velcro* is obtainable from haberdashers and department stores; metal bars (see below) are obtainable from ironmongers and some hardware shops.

To make the blocks
If any off-cuts are too large, secure with the G-clamp and saw to a manageable size.
Sandpaper each block, removing all rough and sharp edges.
Cut and stick a small piece of masking tape to one surface of each block: for the smallest pieces use masking tape 6mm (1/4in.) square, and for the larger ones 13mm (1/2in.) square.

To make the base
Sandpaper the softwood all over.
Clamp the metal strip, mark, drill and countersink two holes 19mm (3/4in.) and 51mm (2in.) in from one end.
Secure the metal strip in the vice and gently bend into a curved shape.
Using the impact adhesive, completely cover the metal strip with *Velcro*. When dry, screw into the softwood base.

Finishing
Apply wood primer to each block. When dry apply two coats of gloss paint, leaving them to dry in a dust free area.
Peel the masking tape off each block and attach pieces of *Velcro* to the unpainted areas, using the impact adhesive.

Adhesive block toy, height 457mm (18in.)

PARANA PINE PUZZLE

Tools
Tenon saw, G-clamp, ruler, pencil, small paint brush

Materials
Parana pine 457mm x 19mm x 305mm (18in. x ¾in. x 12in.)
Fine and medium grade sandpaper
Clear polyurethane varnish
Paper

This elegant puzzle is easy to make but deceptively difficult to put together again. Choose a wood with an attractive grain.

To make the puzzle
Smooth and clean the wood with sandpaper, sanding in the direction of the grain.

Work out a design on paper using straight lines, then transfer this onto the wood using the ruler and pencil.

Secure the wood with the clamp and saw into sections.

Try to be as accurate as possible when sawing, straight lines make the pieces more pleasing to the eye.

Clean and smooth all edges with sandpaper.

Finishing
Varnish each piece and leave to dry in a dust free area.

MAP JIGSAWS

Small British Isles Jigsaw

Tools
Fretsaw with spare blades, G-clamp, drill with 1mm ($\frac{1}{16}$in.) bit, small paint brush, scissors, ruler, pencil

Materials
Plywood, 3mm ($\frac{1}{8}$in.) thick, 305mm x 305mm (12in. x 12in.)
Blockboard, 13mm ($\frac{1}{2}$in.) thick, 305mm x 305mm (12in. x 12in.)
Map of the British Isles
Wood stain
Paper glue
Impact adhesive (such as *Evostik*)
Clear polyurethane varnish
Fine and medium grade sandpaper

The divisions on this map were made by linking the major rivers to one another. Try making jigsaws from several different countries, using political or geographical borders to make the divisions.

To make the map
Cut out the map with scissors, and glue it onto the plywood using paper glue.
Divide the map into about fifteen sections with the pencil (see photograph).
To attach the fretsaw, drill a 1mm ($\frac{1}{16}$in.) hole in the plywood; saw around the map, then saw into sections, securing the plywood pieces with a clamp whenever possible.
Mount the surround onto the blockboard using the impact adhesive.
Peel off the paper map from each puzzle piece.
Clean the surround and puzzle pieces with sandpaper.

Finishing
Apply the wood stain to the puzzle pieces.
Apply varnish to the surround.

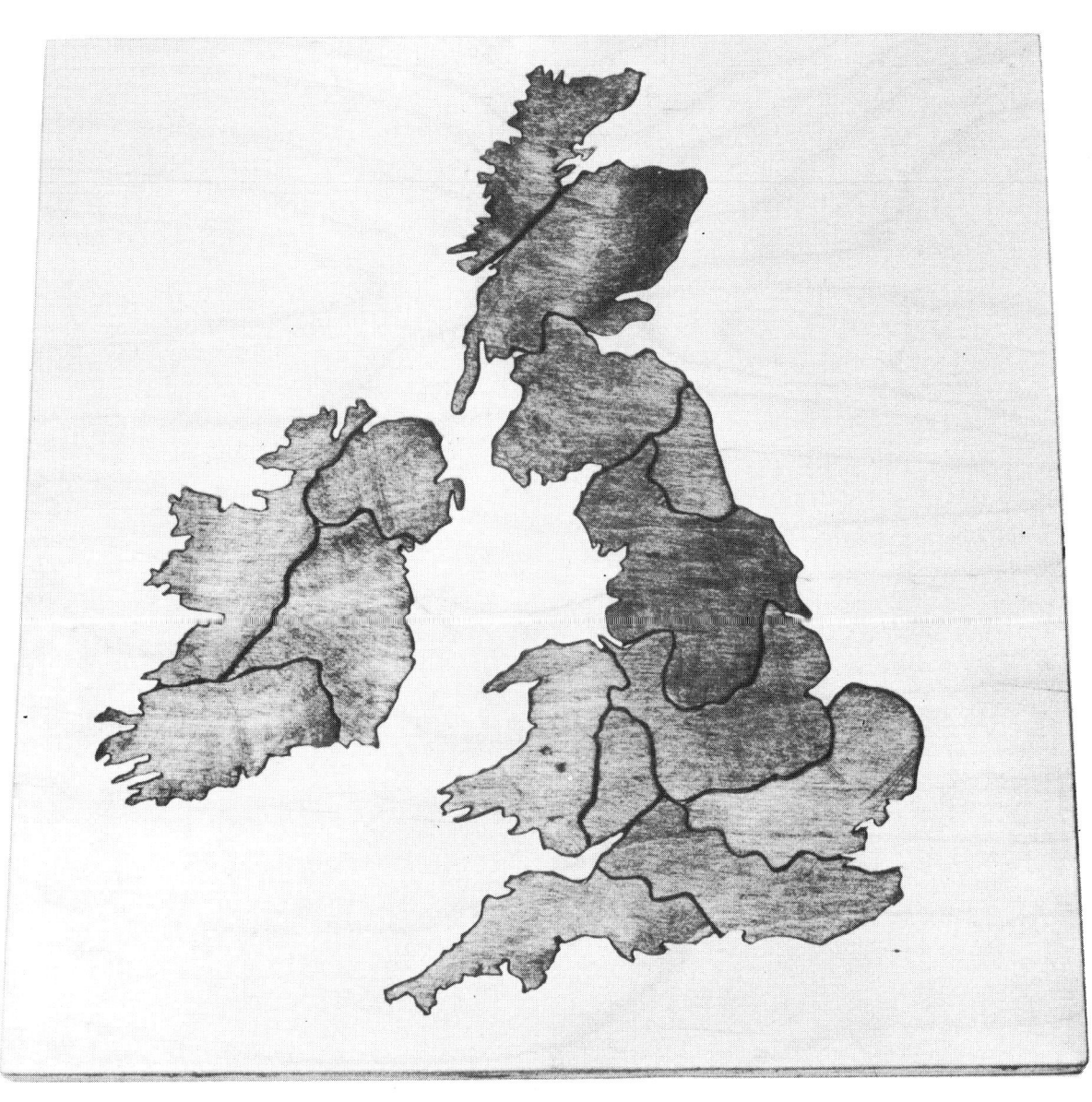

Small British Isles puzzle,
305mm x 305mm (12in. x
12in.)

Large British Isles Jigsaw

Tools
Fretsaw with spare medium teeth blades, G-clamp, drill with 2mm ($^3/_{32}$ in.) bit, scissors, small paint brush, ruler, pencil

Materials
Plywood, 3mm ($^1/_8$ in.) thick, 900mm x 470mm (35$^1/_2$ in. x 18$^1/_2$ in.)
Blockboard, 13mm ($^1/_2$ in.) thick, 900mm x 470mm (35$^1/_2$ in. x 18$^1/_2$ in.)
Map of the British Isles
Assortment of wood stains
Impact adhesive (such as *Evostik*)
Paper glue
Fine and medium grade sandpaper

This impressive puzzle is well worth the time and patience necessary to make it. Each piece represents a different county. For a political version of the map add the county names using rub-on transfer lettering such as *Letraset.*

To make the map
Cut out the map with the scissors, and glue it onto the plywood using paper glue.
Divide the map into county boundaries with the pencil.
To attach the fretsaw, drill a 2mm ($^3/_{32}$ in.) hole in the plywood. Saw around the map, then saw into sections, securing the plywood pieces with a clamp whenever possible.
Mount the surround onto the blockboard using the impact adhesive.
Peel off the paper map from each puzzle piece.
Clean the surround and puzzle pieces with sandpaper.

Finishing
Apply dark wood stain to the map base, and a light stain to the surround.
Apply other colour stains to the puzzle pieces, mixing stains together to obtain different tones.

Large British Isles puzzle,
900mm x 470mm (35½in. x
(18½in.)

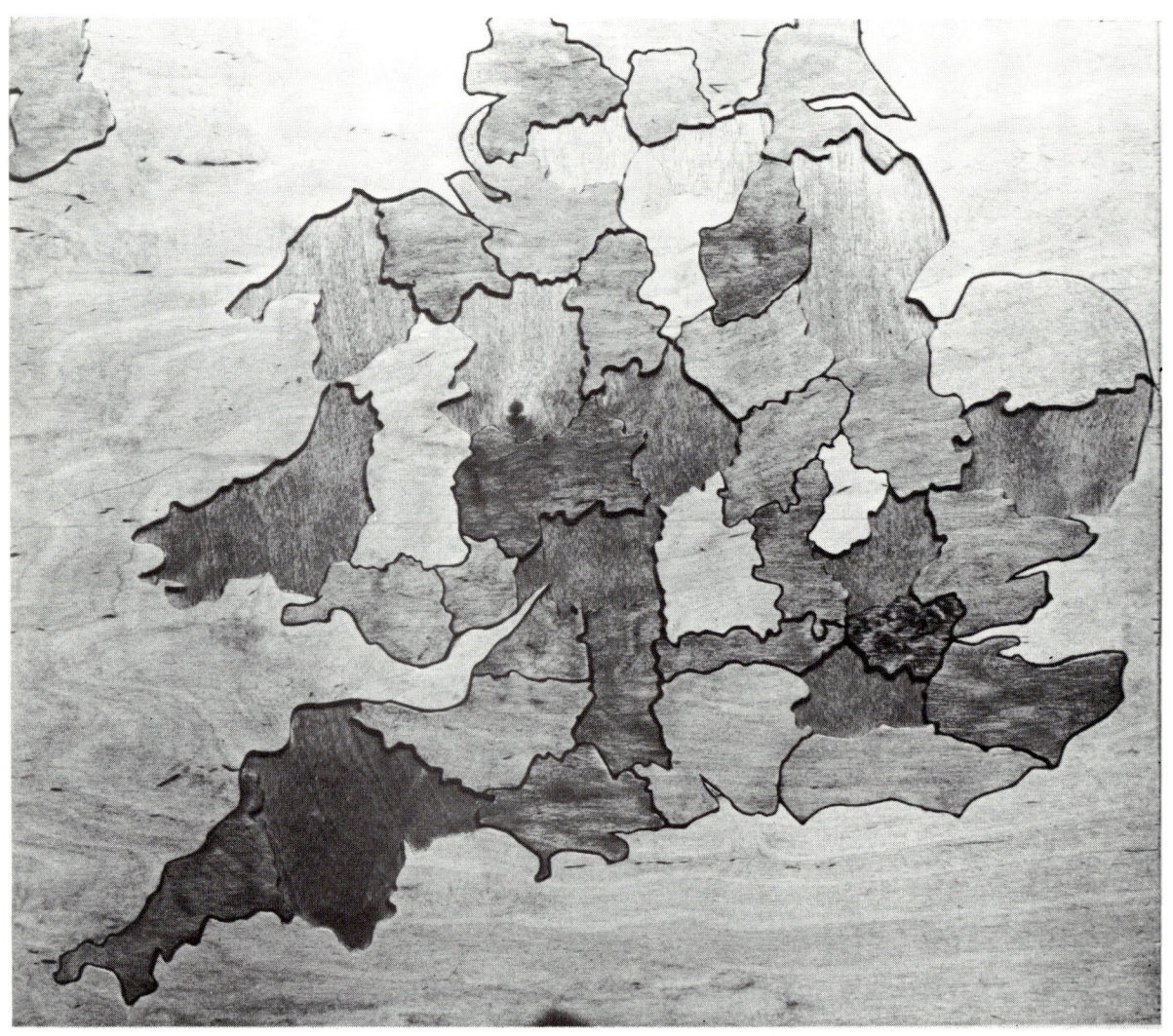

Detail of large puzzle with
pieces removed

Figure 11 Engine measure-
ments

TRAIN

Tools

Tenon saw, G-clamp or vice, try-square, drill with 3mm (1/8 in.) and 1mm (1/32 in.) bits, small screwdriver, pliers, ruler, pencil

Materials

Wooden batten, 51mm x 25mm x 325mm (2in. x 1in. x 12¾in.)
Wooden batten, 25mm x 25mm x 133mm (1in. x 1in. x 5¼in.)
Dowel rod, 19mm (¾in.) diameter; length 305mm (12in.)
Dowel rod, 6mm (¼in.) diameter
28 round-headed screws, 16mm (⅝in.)
7 small eyelets
Wood glue
Fine and medium grade sandpaper

Make as many different carriages as you like to be pulled along by this friendly engine. The whole train set can be painted with brightly coloured non-toxic gloss paint; for a finishing touch paint a name on the side of the engine.

To make the engine

Using the try-square, ruler and pencil, transfer the measurements in figure 11 to the wooden batten and dowel.
Secure with the G-clamp and saw into sections.
Assemble the engine using wood glue.
When dry, drill a 3mm (1/8 in.) hole and push in the chimney.
Sandpaper all over, removing rough and sharp edges.

To make the coal truck

Mark, clamp and saw a 32mm (1¼in.) length of 51mm (2in.) batten.
Mark the position of the wheels 5mm (³⁄₁₆in.) up and 13mm (½in.) in from each end.
Sandpaper all over, removing rough and sharp edges.

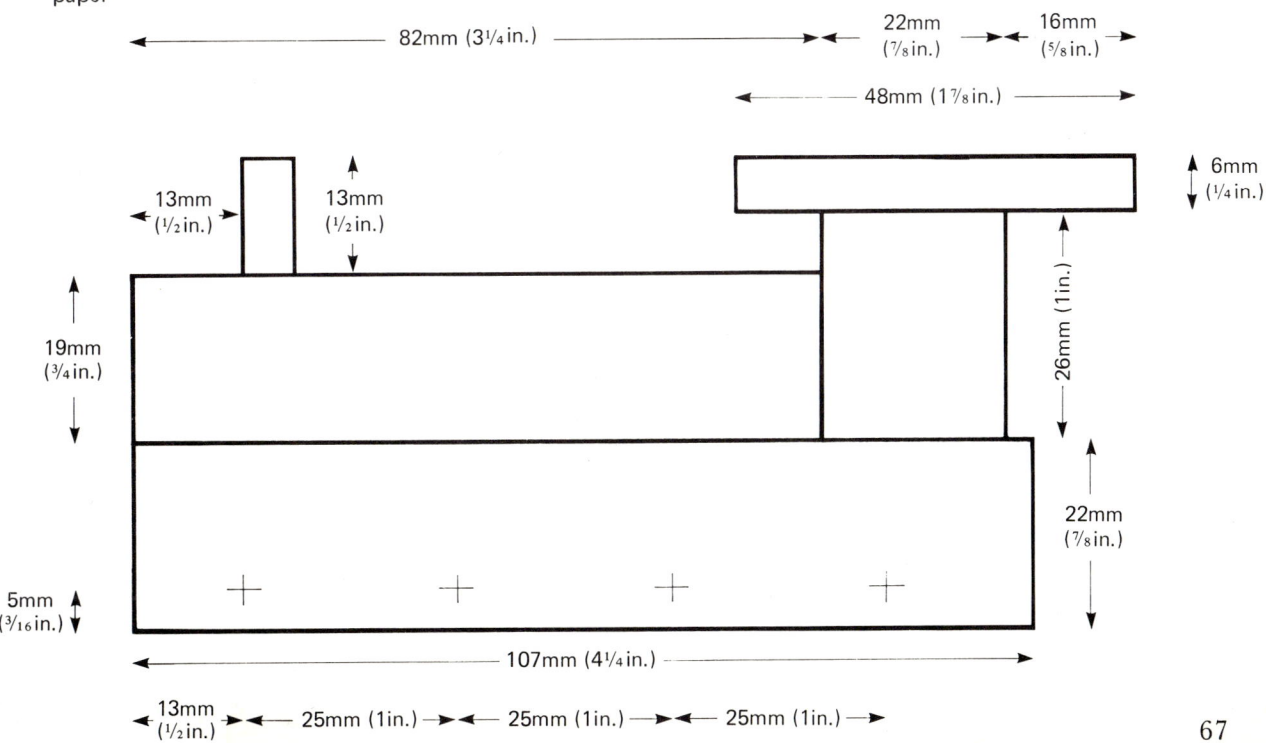

*Train and carriages, length
457mm (18in.)*

To make the carriages
Mark, clamp and saw the remainder of the 51mm (2in.) batten in half.
Mark the position of the wheels 5mm ($^3/_{16}$ in.) up, 13mm ($^1/_2$ in.) and 38mm (1$^1/_2$ in.) in from each end.
Sandpaper all over, removing rough and sharp edges.

To make the wheels
Divide the 16mm ($^5/_8$ in.) dowel into 28 sections, 8mm ($^5/_{16}$ in.) each. Wrap masking tape around the dowel and saw.
Secure each piece in the vice and drill a 3mm ($^1/_8$ in.) hole through the centre.
Attach the wheels to all parts of the train, screwing loosely so that they can rotate freely.

Finishing
Screw an eyelet to both ends of each part, opening one end using the pliers.

MAZE

Tools

Tenon saw, G-clamp or vice, try-square, brace with 19mm (¾in.) bit, mitre board, bradawl, ruler, pencil

Materials

Wooden batten, 51mm x 25mm x 1657mm (2in. x 1in. x 66in.)
Plywood, 3mm (⅛in.) thick, 305mm x 360mm (12in. x 14in.)
Four mirror clips with screws
Wood glue
Wood primer
Brightly coloured gloss paint
Small wooden ball or a marble
Fine and medium grade sandpaper

When constructing this maze make sure that you glue it together securely, as it will be shaken with great vigour. To start play, place a marble in the circular hole and try to shake it out through the arch. The maze has a detachable lid because it is so difficult to get the marble out that many people become convinced it is impossible, and insist on looking inside the box.

To make the maze

Divide the wooden batten into the following lengths using the try-square, ruler and pencil: two measuring 305mm (12in.), two measuring 178mm (7in.). Clamp and saw into sections.
Using the brace, drill a 19mm (¾in.) hole at a central point 38mm (1½in.) in from one end of each shorter length.
Draw a right-angled line on either side of one of the circles, changing the circle into an arch (see photograph).
Clamp and saw.
Mitre the ends of each piece and glue them together to form a rectangle, with the hole and arch diagonally opposed.
Divide and saw the plywood into two sections, both measuring

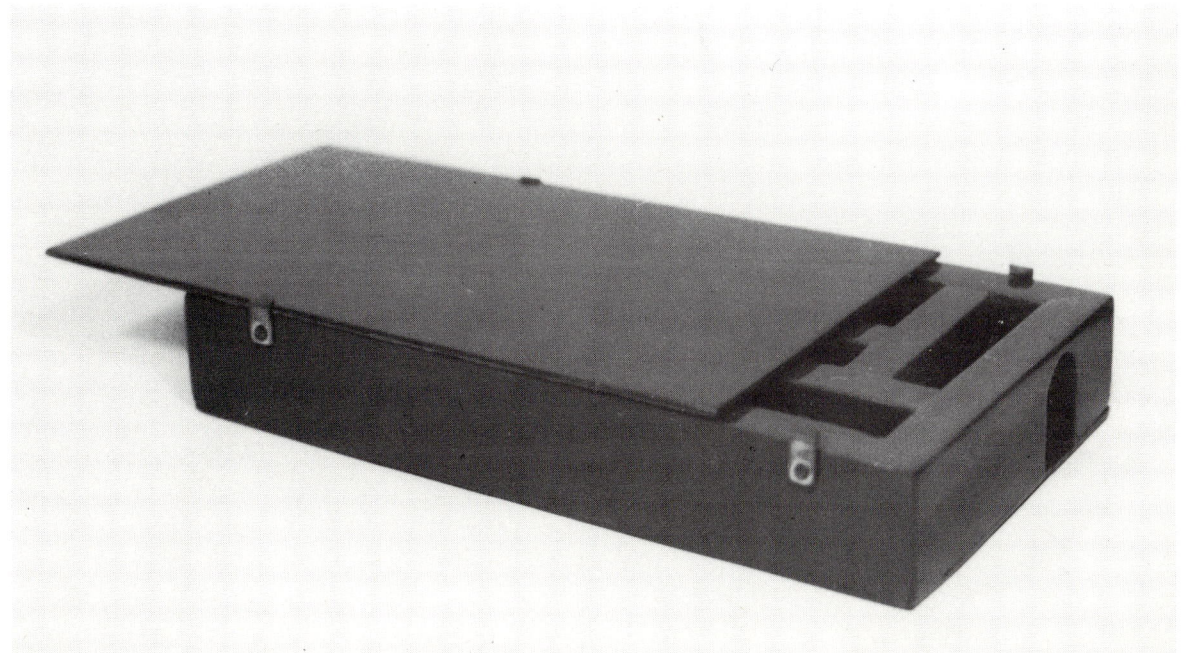

305mm x 178mm (12in. x 7in.); glue the bottom of the maze into place.

Divide the remaining batten into the following lengths: one measuring 264mm (10⅜in.), three measuring 90mm (3½in.), one measuring 51mm (2in.). Clamp and saw into sections.

Mark a 22mm (⅞in.) square in one corner of each 90mm (3½in.) length; clamp and saw.

Sandpaper all parts of the maze removing rough and sharp edges.

Assemble the pieces inside the rectangle using all the square off-cuts as extra obstacles: glue each piece securely to the base.

Finishing

Paint all parts of the maze with wood primer.

When dry apply a brightly coloured gloss paint.

Place the lid on the maze and mark two holes in each of the two longer sides, 38mm (1½in.) from the corners.

Start the screw holes with the bradawl and loosely screw the mirror clips into place so that the lid can slide off.

Maze, 305mm x 178mm (12in. x 7in.)

MILITARY TANK

This army tank has a revolving turret, and can be painted in a green and khaki camouflage pattern.

To make the tank

Divide the batten into two lengths measuring 76mm (3in.) and 44mm (1¾in.); clamp and saw.

Drill to a depth of 13mm (½in.) in the top centre of each piece.

To accommodate the barrel, mark the centre of the side of the turret and drill a hole 13mm (½in.) deep.

Using the 6mm (¼in.) dowel, saw the barrel 76mm (3in.) and the pivot 25mm (1in.).

Sandpaper all over removing rough and sharp edges.

Join the turret to the body by pushing the shorter length of dowel into the holes.

Push the barrel into the side of the turret, using wood glue if it feels loose.

To make the wheels

Divide the 25mm (1in.) dowel into four 5mm (⅕in.) sections.

Wrap masking tape around the dowel and saw.

Secure each piece in the vice and drill a 3mm (⅛in.) hole through the centre.

Sand the edges with sandpaper.

To attach the wheels to the body, measure 13mm (½in.) in and 6mm (¼in.) up the side: start the screw-holes with the bradawl.

Attach the screws loosely so that the wheels can rotate freely.

Finishing

Apply clear polyurethane varnish, or paint if desired.

Tools
Tenon saw, drill with 3mm (⅛in.) and 6mm (¼in.) bits, bradawl, small screwdriver, try-square, vice or G-clamp, pencil, ruler

Materials
Wooden batten, 50mm x 25mm x 120mm (2in. x 1in. x 4¾in.)
Dowel rod, 6mm (¼in.) diameter
Dowel rod, 25mm (1in.) diameter
Four 13mm (½in.) round-headed screws
Wood glue
Fine and medium grade sandpaper

Tank with revolving turret,
length 76mm (3in.)

PENCIL AND RULER BOX

Tools
Tenon saw, G-clamp or vice, try-square, Stanley knife, small paint brush, ruler, pencil

Materials
Plywood, 10mm (⅜in.) thick, 407mm x 325mm (16in. x 12¾in.)
Softwood 51mm x 51mm x 63mm (2in. x 2in. x 2½in.)
Light and dark veneers
Wood glue
Impact adhesive (such as *Evostik*)
Gloss polyurethane varnish
Fine and medium grade sandpaper

An unusual and attractive pencil box which has a split-level interior. The pencils stand on a central block while the rulers slide down the side.

To make the box
Divide the plywood into the following sizes using the try-square, ruler and pencil: four pieces measuring 152mm x 82mm (6in. x 3¼ in.), one piece measuring 102mm x 82mm (4in. x 3¼ in.). Clamp and saw into sections.

Pencil and ruler box, height 152mm (6in.)

Apply wood glue to the edges of the sides and construct the box shape using butt joints; when dry, glue the bottom into position. Using the Stanley knife cut strips of veneer 32mm (1¼in.) wide. Glue the strips diagonally across each side of the box, covering one side at a time: as each side is completed, trim away excess veneer using the Stanley knife.

Cover the bottom with veneer strips. Cut 10mm (³⁄₈in.) strips for the top edges of the box, and glue into place (see photograph).

Glue the softwood inside the base of the box using wood glue; leave equal gaps between the block and the box to accommodate rulers.

Finishing
Apply gloss varnish, completely covering the box.

Animal on wheels, length 178mm (7in.)

ANIMAL ON WHEELS

Tools
Tenon saw, coping saw, G-clamp or vice, drill with 1mm (¹⁄₁₆in.) and 3mm (¹⁄₈in.) bits, small round file, scissors, ruler, pencil

Materials
Plywood, 19mm (¾in.) thick, 178mm x 140mm (7in. x 5½in.)
Dowel rod, 38mm (1½in.) diameter, *or* four ready-made wheels
Paper glue
Dark wood stain
Four 25mm (1in.) round-headed screws
Masking tape
Fine and medium grade sand-paper

This animal (known as 'the critter') has ready-made wheels bought from a shop, but you can easily make your own. For the younger child, screw an eyelet in the front of the animal and attach string so that it can be pulled along. Other favourite animals can be made by tracing their shapes from books and magazines.

To make the animal
Draw or trace out an animal shape from a magazine onto paper, making sure that its feet or hooves are wide enough to accommodate the screws.
Cut out the shape using scissors, and glue it to the plywood.
Secure the plywood with the G-clamp, and saw round the outline using the coping saw.
Peel off the paper, and sandpaper all over removing rough and sharp edges.

Clamp and add texture to the body using the file.
Drill a 1mm ($\frac{1}{16}$in.) hole in the bottom of each leg to accommodate the screws.

To make the wheels
Divide the dowel into four 13mm ($\frac{1}{2}$in.) sections.
Wrap masking tape around the dowel and saw.
Secure each piece in the vice and drill a 3mm ($\frac{1}{8}$in.) hole through the centre.
Attach the screws loosely so that the wheels can rotate freely.

Finishing
Apply a dark wood stain, or paint the animal in the appropriate colours, and mark on the facial features.

GUN-BOAT

Tools
Coping saw, G-clamp or vice, drill with 10mm (³⁄₈in.) and 3mm (¹⁄₈in.) bits, pencil

Materials
Softwood 51mm x 51mm x 229mm (2in. x 2in. x 9in.)
Wooden batten 51mm x 25mm x 57mm (2in. x 1in. x 2¹⁄₄in.)
Three dowel off-cuts for the chimney and guns
Wood glue

Gun-boat, length 229mm (9in.)

This boat is designed to be played with on a dry surface. If you wish to float it on water, assemble it using screws instead of wood glue, as water would quickly destroy the glue's adhesive properties.

To make the boat
Draw the body shape of the boat on the softwood; secure with the G-clamp and saw the drawn shapes off each end.
Glue the dowel and batten on top to form the cabin and chimney.
When dry, secure the boat with the G-clamp and drill four 3mm (¹⁄₈in.) holes, 6mm (¹⁄₄in.) apart, in the two sides of the cabin.
Drill two holes angled downwards in the front of the cabin: push in two short lengths of dowel to form the guns.
Drill a 10mm (³⁄₈in.) hole in the top of the chimney.
Sandpaper all over removing all rough and sharp edges.

Finishing
Varnish all over, or paint the boat a battleship grey.

ROBOTS

Simple Robot

Tools
Tenon saw, G-clamp or vice,
drill with 6mm (¼ in.) bit,
ruler, pencil

Materials
Wooden off-cuts of varying
size and shape, including
square and rectangular blocks,
large diameter dowel rod, and
6mm (¼ in.) diameter dowel
rod
Wood glue
Masking tape
Fine and medium grade sandpaper

This small robot with movable arms is made from wooden off-cuts.
No specific sizes and shapes are given, because they will depend on
the off-cuts you have available. Experiment with various shapes first
to see what looks most like a robot.

To make the robot
Mark, clamp and saw any off-cut that is too large or has an uneven
edge.
Sandpaper all parts to be used removing rough and sharp edges, and
ensuring that the feet will hold the robot steady.
Clamp and drill a 6mm (¼ in.) hole through the upper part of the
body and through one end of both the dowel pieces which are to be
used for the arms.
Push the 6mm (¼ in.) dowel through the body and attach the arms.
Attach the head and legs using wood glue.

Finishing
Apply clear polyurethane varnish.

*Simple robot, height 140mm
(5½ in.)*

Robot Family

These striking toys have movable arms, and the two larger robots
have hinged lids and so can be used as storage boxes. Add a touch of
luxury by lining the box interiors and soles of the feet with coloured
felt.

Tools

Tenon saw, G-clamp or vice, try-square, drill with 1mm ($\frac{1}{32}$ in.) and 6mm ($\frac{1}{4}$ in.) bits, 13mm ($\frac{1}{2}$ in.) chisel, small screwdriver, small paint brush, ruler, pencil

Materials

Plywood, 10mm ($\frac{3}{8}$ in.) thick, 407mm x 305mm (16in. x 12in.)
Softwood, 51mm x 51mm x 254mm (2in. x 2in. x 10in.)
Dowel rod, 25mm (1in.) diameter, 686mm (27in.)
Dowel rod, 32mm ($1\frac{1}{4}$in.) diameter, 457mm (18in.)
Dowel rod, 16mm ($\frac{5}{8}$in.) diameter, 305mm (12in.)
Dowel rod, 6mm ($\frac{1}{4}$in.) diameter, 305mm (12in.)
Dowel rod, 9mm ($\frac{3}{8}$in.) diameter, 152mm (6in.)
Dowel rod, 38mm ($1\frac{1}{2}$in.) diameter, 51mm (2in.)
Half round rod, 9mm ($\frac{3}{8}$in.) wide, 178mm (7in.)
Two 38mm ($1\frac{1}{2}$in.) brass hinges with screws
Wood primer
Silver paint
Wood glue
Fine and medium grade sandpaper

To make the mother and father

Divide the plywood into the following sizes using the try-square, ruler, and pencil: two fronts and two backs 102mm x 82mm (4in. x $3\frac{1}{4}$in.); four sides 102mm x 63mm (4in. x $2\frac{1}{2}$in.); two lids 82mm x 82mm ($3\frac{1}{4}$in. x $3\frac{1}{4}$in.); two bottoms 63mm x 63mm ($2\frac{1}{2}$in. x $2\frac{1}{2}$in.). Clamp and saw into sections.

Apply wood glue to the side edges and construct the two box shapes using butt joints. When dry, glue the bottom pieces into position.

Join the lids to the boxes with the brass hinges (see figure 3 page 15). Divide and saw the half round rod in half, and glue it to the front of the lids.

Mark a central point 32mm ($1\frac{1}{4}$in.) down the two sides of each box; clamp and drill 6mm ($\frac{1}{4}$in.) holes at the marked points.

Divide the 6mm ($\frac{1}{4}$in.) dowel into four 38mm ($1\frac{1}{2}$in.) lengths; clamp, saw, and secure the lengths in the drill holes using wood glue.

To make the arms, divide the 25mm (1in.) dowel into four 102mm (4in.) lengths; clamp and saw.

Clamp and drill a 6mm ($\frac{1}{4}$in.) hole 35mm ($1\frac{3}{8}$in.) down each arm. Push onto (but do not glue) the 6mm ($\frac{1}{4}$in.) dowel.

To make the legs and necks divide the 32mm ($1\frac{1}{4}$in.) dowel into four 102mm (4in.) lengths and two 16mm ($\frac{5}{8}$in.) lengths; clamp and saw.

Glue the legs underneath the centre of the boxes, 6mm ($\frac{1}{4}$in.) in from the sides.

Calculate the centre of each lid and attach the necks using wood glue.

To make the heads and feet, divide the softwood into the following sizes: two measuring 51mm x 51mm x 70mm (2in. x 2in. x $2\frac{3}{4}$in.) and two measuring 51mm x 51mm x 19mm (2in. x 2in. x $\frac{3}{4}$in.).

Glue the heads and square feet (for the male robot) into place.

For the female feet divide the 38mm ($1\frac{1}{2}$in.) dowel in half; clamp, saw, and glue into place.

Sandpaper both robots all over, removing rough and sharp edges.

To decorate the robots

Divide the 16mm ($\frac{5}{8}$in.) and 25mm (1in.) dowel rod into 34 discs, each 6mm ($\frac{1}{4}$in.) thick; clamp and saw.

To make the male eyes cut two 19mm ($\frac{3}{4}$in.) squares 6mm ($\frac{1}{4}$in.) thick; clamp and saw.

Sandpaper all the pieces, removing any sharp edges.

Glue the pieces onto each robot (see photograph).

To make the baby robot
Construct the baby in the same way, using the remaining pieces of wood, and following the instructions for the small off-cut robot on page 81.

Finishing
Apply wood primer to all three robots.
Cover with silver paint applying two coats if necessary.
If desired, line the inside of the boxes and the soles of the feet with felt.

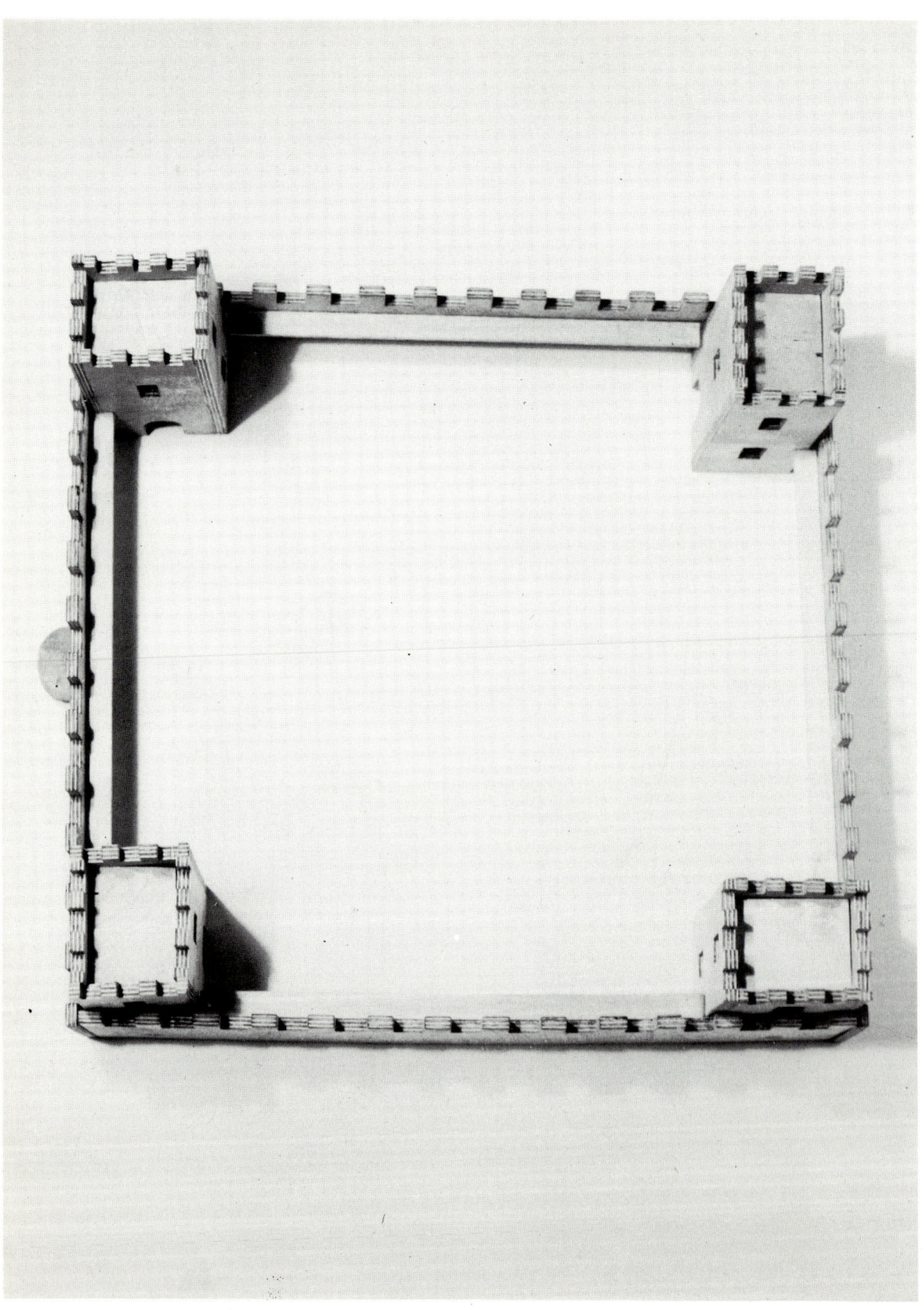

CASTLE

Tools
Tenon saw, coping saw, G-clamps or vice, try-square, drill with 3mm (1/8in.) bit, brace with 13mm (1/2in.) bit, hammer, small round file, paint brush, ruler, pencil

Materials
Plywood, 10mm (3/8in.) thick, 915mm x 534mm (36in. x 21in.)
Wooden batten, 6mm x 19mm x 1372mm (1/4in. x 3/4in. x 54in.)
Dowel rod, 13mm (1/2in.) diameter
Dowel rod, 6mm (1/4in.) diameter
Plywood, 3mm (1/8in.) thick, (for the drawbridge)
Two small staples
Masking tape
Wood stains
Wood glue
Fine and medium grade sandpaper

This mediaeval castle has a movable drawbridge and dismantles easily for convenient storage. The four walls and keeps are constructed as separate pieces, and quickly slot into one another to form the completed castle. It is designed to be used with plastic soldiers which are available from most toy and model shops. This basic plan could easily be adapted to make a U.S. cavalry fort, or even a prison.

To make the castle walls
Divide the plywood into four 102mm x 534mm (4in. x 21in.) lengths using the try-square, ruler and pencil; clamp and saw into sections.
Draw a line 19mm (3/4in.) wide along one side of each length, and divide into 19mm (3/4in.) squares.
Drill a 3mm (1/8in.) hole in the corner of every alternate square. Attach the coping saw and cut out.
To make the drawbridge entrance mark a 51mm (2in.) square in the centre of the base of one of the walls, curving the top of the square. Cut out using the coping saw.
Sandpaper the walls all over removing rough and sharp edges.

To make the keeps
Divide the remaining plywood into sixteen 178mm x 76mm (7in. x 3in.) sections; clamp and saw.
Draw a line 13mm (1/2in.) wide along one shorter side on each piece. Mark along the line 6mm (1/4in.) then divide into 13mm (1/2in.) squares.
Drill a hole into the corner of every alternate square; attach the coping saw and cut out.
Draw in the windows and doorways on each keep; secure each piece and cut out using a coping saw.
Construct the keeps using butt joints: apply wood glue to the edges of the sides and clamp until dry.
To make the keep ceilings, mark, clamp and saw four pieces measuring 76mm x 57mm (3in. x 2 1/4in.), and glue them into place.
When dry, sandpaper each keep all over.
To attach the keeps to the walls, clamp the wall flush with one side of the keep and drill a 13mm (1/2in.) hole through both thicknesses. Repeat this, but when drilling the other two sides remember to allow for the thickness of the adjoining wall.
Saw eight 25mm (1in.) lengths of 13mm (1/2in.) diameter dowel rod and insert into the wall, gluing if necessary.

Castle, 554mm x 534mm (21 3/4in. x 21in.)

To make the battlements and drawbridge

Construct the castle, then mark and measure the distances between each keep. Transfer these measurements to the wooden batten; clamp and saw into sections.

Dismantle the castle and glue the lengths into place, about 38mm (1½in.) down the inside of the castle walls. (This depends on the size of your model soldiers.)

Transfer the drawbridge shape onto the 3mm (⅛in.) plywood. Clamp and cut out using the coping saw.

Glue a 90mm (3½in.) length of 6mm (¼in.) diameter dowel onto the bottom of the drawbridge, leaving equal amounts showing on each side.

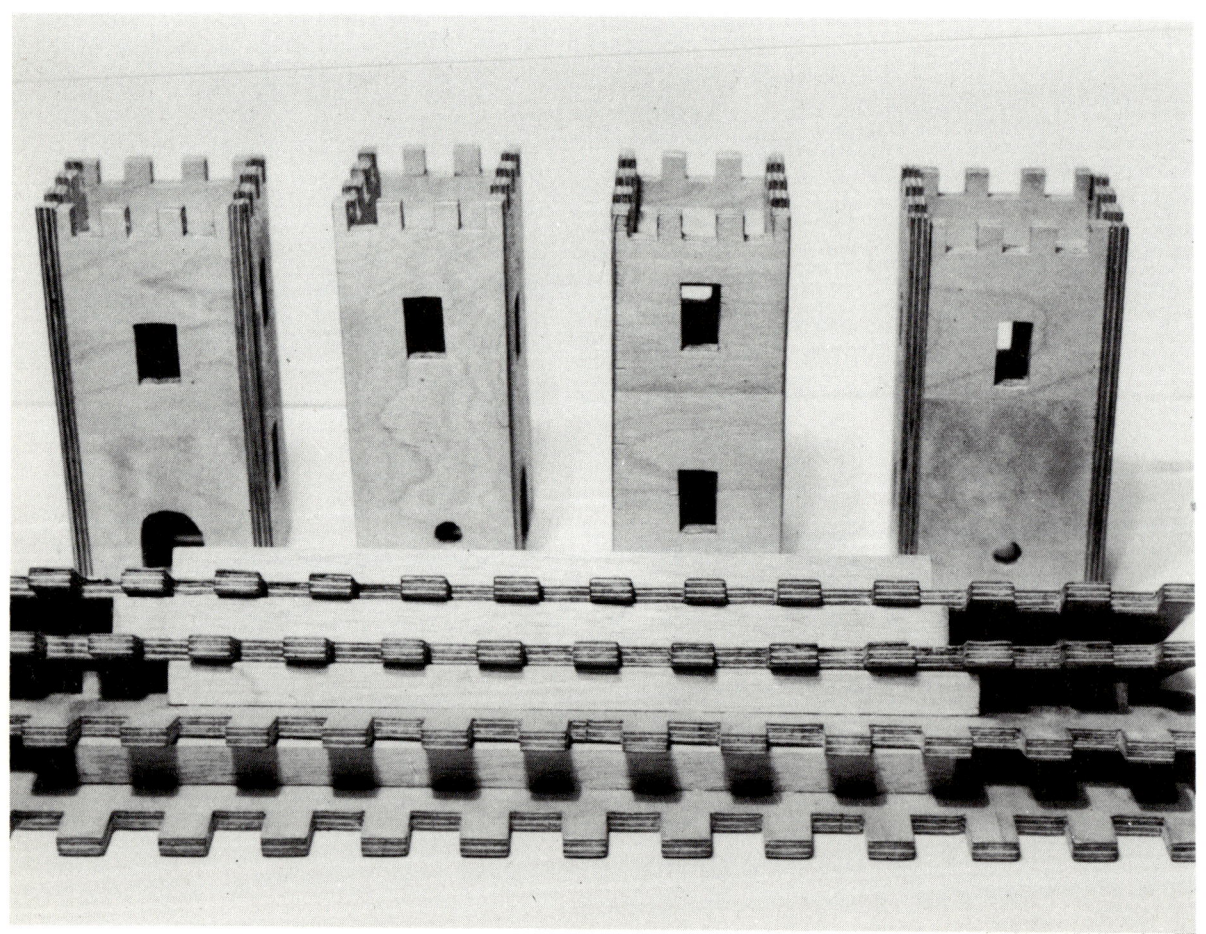

File a groove all round the dowel, 10mm (³⁄₈ in.) in from each end. Push the staples over the grooves and fix to the inside of the wall using the hammer.

Finishing
Apply a light oak wood stain to all pieces. Use a darker stain for the drawbridge, if desired.

To transform the castle into a United States cavalry fort, texture the walls and the towers with a file or thin chisel to resemble long wooden logs, and paint them a dark brown colour. Instead of a drawbridge, make double gates which open sideways instead of downwards.

SUPPLIERS

Plywood, softwood, wooden batten and dowel rod can be obtained from most timber merchants. Masking tape, sandpaper, adhesives, paints, eyelets, screws, wood stains, white spirit and hinges may be obtained from most hardware stores and large department stores such as Woolworths, John Lewis, Selfridges and Debenhams.

Hardwood and softwood

F H Norman and Co. Ltd
26 Warner Street
London EC1

Latchford
61 Endall Street
London WC2

C F Anderson and Son Ltd
Islington Green
London N1

Jones Brothers
50 Turnham Green Terrace
London W4

Wooden balls, ready-made wheels and wood

Frank Romany Ltd
52 Camden High Street
London NW1

R W Dunn and Son
183 Shepherds Bush Market
London W12

Collins and Son
Earlham Street
London WC2

FURTHER READING

How to Start Using Tools
Charles Graveney
Cassell Collier Macmillan,
London

Using Woodworking Tools
Edward Wynter
A & C Black Ltd., London

Carpentry is Easy
Marshall Cavendish Ltd.,
London

Simple Wooden Toy Designs
Mike Smith
Stanley Paul Ltd., London

Toys from Wood
Edited by Peter Scaife
Evans Brothers Ltd., London

Plywood
Rolf Hartung
B T Batsford, London

Furniture for Children
Brian Brooks
Evans Brothers Ltd., London

Wood Appliqué
Jean Ray Laury
Van Nostrand Reinhold,
London

Creative Woodcraft
Ernst Rottger
B T Batsford, London

INDEX